The bronze statue of Confucius in the Yushima Seido, a Confucian temple in Tokyo, said to have been brought from the Confucian Temple of Ch'ü-fou by a Chinese exile during the Ming dynasty.

CONFUCIUS
His Life and Thought

Shigeki Kaizuka

Translated by Geoffrey Bownas

DOVER PUBLICATIONS, INC.
Mineola, New York

Bibliographical Note

This Dover edition, first published in 2002, is an unabridged republication of *Confucius*, translated from the Japanese by Geoffrey Bownas, and originally published by George Allen & Unwin, Ltd., London, and the Macmillan Company, New York, in 1956, as No. 17 in the series "Ethical and Religious Classics of East and West."

Library of Congress Cataloging-in-Publication Data

Kaizuka, Shigeki, 1904–
    Confucius : his life and thought / Shigeki Kaizuka ; translated by Geoffrey Bownas.—Dover ed.
        p. cm.
    Originally published: London : G. Allen & Unwin ; New York : Macmillan Co., 1956, in series: Ethical and religious classics of East and West.
    Includes index.
    ISBN 0-486-42139-2 (pbk.)
     1. Confucius. I. Title.

B128.C8 K32 2002
181'.112—dc21
[B]

2002019393

Manufactured in the United States of America
Dover Publications, Inc., 31 East 2nd Street, Mineola, N.Y. 11501

GENERAL INTRODUCTION

AS A RESULT of two Wars that have devastated the World men and women everywhere feel a twofold need. We need a deeper understanding and appreciation of other peoples and their civilizations, especially their moral and spiritual achievements. And we need a wider vision of the Universe, a clearer insight into the fundamentals of ethics and religion. How ought men to behave? How ought nations? Does God exist? What is His Nature? How is He related to His creation? Especially, how can man approach Him? In other words, there is a general desire to know what the greatest minds, whether of East or West, have thought and said about the Truth of God and of the beings who (as most of them hold) have sprung from Him, live by Him, and return to Him.

It is the object of this Series, which originated among a group of Oxford men and their friends, to place the chief ethical and religious masterpieces of the world, both Christian and non-Christian, within easy reach of the intelligent reader who is not necessarily an expert— the ex-Service man who is interested in the East, the undergraduate, the adult student, the intelligent public generally. The Series will contain books of three kinds: translations, reproductions of ideal and religious art, and background books showing the surroundings in which the literature and art arose and developed. These books overlap each other. Religious art, both in East and West, often illustrates a religious text, and in suitable cases the text and the pictures will be printed together to complete each other. The background books will often consist largely of translations. The volumes will be prepared by scholars of distinction, who will try to make them, not only scholarly, but intelligible and enjoyable. This Introduction represents the views of the General Editors as to the scope of the Series, but not necessarily the views of all contributors to it. The contents of the books will also be very varied—ethical and social, biographical, devotional, philosophic and mystical, whether in poetry, in pictures or in prose. There is a great wealth of material. Confucius lived in a time much like our own, when State was at war with State and the people suffering and disillusioned; and the 'Classics' he preserved or inspired show the social virtues that may unite families, classes and States into one great family, in obedience to the Will of Heaven. Asoka and Akbar (both of them great patrons of art) ruled a vast Empire on the principles of religious faith. There are the moral anecdotes and moral maxims of the Jewish and Muslim writers of the Middle Ages. There are the beautiful tales of courage, love and fidelity in the Indian and Persian epics. Shakespeare's plays show that he thought the true relation between man and man is love. Here and there a volume will illustrate the unethical or less ethical man and difficulties that beset him.

Then there are the devotional and philosophic works. The lives and legends (legends often express religious truth with clarity and beauty) of the Buddha, of the parents of Mary, of Francis of Assisi, and the exquisite sculptures and paintings that illustrate them. Indian and Christian religious music, and the words of prayer and praise which the music intensifies. There are the prophets and apocalyptic writers, Zarathustrian and Hebrew; the Greek philosophers, Christian thinkers—and the Greek, Latin, medieval and modern—whom they so deeply influenced. There is, too, the Hindu, Buddhist and Christian teaching expressed in such great monuments as the Indian temples, Barabudur (the

6

Chartres of Asia) and Ajanta, Chartres itself and the Sistine Chapel.

Finally, there are the mystics of feeling, and the mystical philosophers. In God-loving India the poets, musicians, sculptors and painters inspired by the spiritual worship of Krishna and Rama, as well as the philosophic mystics from the Upanishads onward. The two great Taoists Lao-tze and Chuang-tze and the Sung mystical painters in China, Rumi and other sufis in Islam, Plato and Plotinus, followed by 'Dionysius', Eckhart, St. John of the Cross and (in our view) Dante and other great mystics and mystical painters in many Christian lands.

Mankind is hungry, but the feast is there, though it is locked up and hidden away. It is the aim of this Series to put it within reach, so that, like the heroes of Homer, we may stretch forth our hands to the good cheer laid before us.

No doubt the great religions differ in fundamental respects. But they are not nearly so far from one another as they seem. We think they are further off than they are largely because we so often misunderstand and misrepresent them. Those whose own religion is dogmatic have often been as ready to learn from other teachings as those who are liberals in religion. Above all, there is an enormous amount of common ground in the great religions, concerning, too, the most fundamental matters. There is frequent agreement on the Divine Nature; God is the One, Self-subsisting Reality, knowing Himself, and therefore loving and rejoicing in Himself. Nature and finite spirits are in some way subordinate kinds of Being, or merely appearances of the Divine, the One. The three stages of the way of man's approach or return to God are in essence the same in Christian and non-Christian teaching: an

7

ethical stage, then one of knowledge and love, leading to the mystical union of the soul with God. Each stage will be illustrated in these volumes.

Something of all this may (it is hoped) be learnt from the books and pictures in this Series. Read and pondered with a desire to learn, they will help men and women to find 'fulness of life', and peoples to live together in greater understanding and harmony. To-day the earth is beautiful, but men are disillusioned and afraid. But there may come a day, perhaps not a distant day, when there will be a renaissance of man's spirit: when men will be innocent and happy amid the beauty of the world, or their eyes will be opened to see that egoism and strife are folly, that the universe is fundamentally spiritual, and that men are the sons of God.

> They shall not hurt nor destroy
> In all My holy mountain:
> For all the earth shall be full of the
> knowledge of the Lord
> As the waters cover the sea.

THE EDITORS

TRANSLATOR'S NOTE

A work by a Japanese about Chinese thought, translated by an Englishman, is the sort of venture of which, I believe, H. N. Spalding would have approved. It is with deep gratitude that I record my sincere appreciation to The Spalding Trust for its help in the publication of this work.

This translation also goes a slight way towards discharging the immense debts I owe to Professor Kaizuka, and to all his staff at Jimbun Kagaku Kenkyūjo (Research Institute of Humanistic Sciences), in Kyōto University, in return for their generous hospitality during a period of study in Japan.

Professor Kaizuka has read the manuscript, and has suggested emendations, but the responsibility for the translation remains mine. I must thank R. S. Dawson, of the Department of Oriental Studies in the University of Durham, and M. G. Brown, of Winchester College, for their many suggestions, W. Taylor, Senior Lecturer of the Oxford School of Architecture, for his maps, and my wife, who throughout has offered valuable help and criticism.

And—perhaps the most important—Michiharu Itō, of Kyōto University, who first sowed the seeds of the idea in a Kyōto coffee-house.

CONTENTS

ONE

THE AGE OF CONFUCIUS

*1 The Historical Significance of the Sixth and
Fifth Centuries B.C.*

Confucius was born in about the year 551 B.C. in the state of Lu, which lay near the modern Ch'ü-fou Prefecture in Shantung Province, and whose ruler was related by blood to the royal house of Chou. Chou's seat lay at Lo-yang, in the modern province of Honan, and the kingdom of Lu was situated at the eastern confines of her realm. Until his death at the age of seventy-four, Confucius made his way round the various kingdoms of eastern China, spreading his own particular theory of government.

Before I describe the condition of China in Confucius' time, it would be expedient to consider the significance of this period for the history of ancient China. The sixth and fifth centuries fall in the latter part of the period in Chinese history which has come to be called the 'Ch'un-ch'iu',—or the 'Spring and Autumn' period. This title derives from the name of the chronicle 'Ch'un-ch'iu' which records the history of these times, and which is said to have been based on the official state annals of Lu, the state to which Confucius belonged. Strictly, the period lasted for 242 years—from 722 to 481 B.C.— during which the authority of the Chou royal court had disintegrated and China had been divided into twelve kingdoms which competed for hegemony. With the rise of repeated internal struggles within these kingdoms, control was gradually usurped by the families who

13

provided candidates for the highest offices of state, and further, the actual authority seemed about to pass to the retainers of such high officials, who, from the eyes of the rulers of the kingdoms, were but arrière-vassals.

Internationally, there prevailed a situation of chronic warfare: within the kingdoms, there were sudden outbreaks of internecine disorder and unhappy ill-starred incidents such as the assassination of the ruler frequently occurred. Confucius, unable to bear to look on this anarchy and lawlessness, is said to have planned to add his own comments to the official state chronicle of Lu, in the hope that, by giving prominence to the conduct of insurgent ministers who slew their princes, and of rebel sons who murdered their fathers, he might induce some spirit of self-examination in the people of the time; hence his resolve to compile the 'Ch'un-ch'iu'.

Whether Confucius did in fact compile the 'Ch'un-ch'iu' has become a matter of considerable doubt for recent scholars, and there are those who would argue that this is no more than a tradition passed on within one sect of Confucianism. The problem of the veracity of this tradition will be discussed in detail later: the very existence of the tradition, however, reveals the age as one in which the organization of strictly defined social ranks of Emperor, lord, minister, senior officer and knight, built on the basis of the system of the Chou royal court—the political and social structure to which we have come to give the name of feudalism—was gradually being dismembered. The several kingdoms which had asserted their independence during this period continued to make war on each other, and in the age that followed, (which lasted from 478 to 220 B.C., and is called 'The Period of the Seven Kingdoms'), they came to be ranged into seven powerful states, and waged war still more savagely, so that this period is also styled 'The

Age of the Warring States'. Finally, as the outcome of this struggle, a unified empire was established in 220 B.C., by Ch'in, a state in the west which had but recently come to the fore, and which had adopted a novel and extremely militaristic form of government, and had enforced a policy of enriching the state and strengthening its military potential.

In her newly established empire, Ch'in did away with the organization hitherto prevailing: dividing the whole realm into districts and the districts further into prefectures, she set up in the district a governor to control civil matters, and a legate in charge of military affairs; in the prefecture was established the resident whose office corresponded to that of the prefect of the present day. Since all such officers were appointed and dispatched to their posts by the Ch'in regime, the Ch'in empire took the form of government by centralized authority, ruling as it did through the medium of officials appointed by this central authority. However, only the highest officials, of the style of the district governor and the prefectural resident, were appointed by the central government, and until the time of the subsequent dynasty, that of the Han, the selection of local officials apart from those in the topmost positions was left to the free choice of the governor, or the resident, and the great majority came from the ranks of local candidates. In this aspect, as a certain degree of understanding was preserved with the powerful families who naturally possessed a strong local influence, the government retained more of a compromise nature, and there still remained a fair amount of local authority. Thus while the tendency to permit a certain degree of local authority persisted, this administrative system put into force by the Ch'in empire, and administered by a centralized bureaucracy, is given the name of 'the

15

district and prefecture system', to distinguish it from the form which preceded it.

This 'district and prefecture' organization was preceded by the regional administrative system of the Chou royal court, in which the realm was divided into countless kingdoms, son succeeding father as ruler on the hereditary principle. The Chou court retained a nominal prerogative of surveillance through the grant of formal recognition of the succession of the feudatory, but in no way interfered in internal administration. The relationship between the feudal lord and his vassals was modelled on the same principle, and this period, to distinguish it from the district and prefectural system of the Ch'in dynasty, has come to be called in China that of the feudal system. In the Ch'un-ch'iu period, the feudalism of the Chou dynasty began gradually to crumble, with the tendency becoming more and more marked in the 'Warring States' period; at this point, the seven great kingdoms began to adopt the district and prefectural administrative system, and this was finally adapted to the entire realm under the unification achieved by Ch'in. The sixth and fifth centuries B.C., corresponding to the later period of the Ch'un-ch'iu, saw a sudden spurt in the process of the disintegration of feudalism, with as yet no emergence of a new administrative machinery to take its place. In the sphere of government, the traditional structure had broken down, and conditions of anarchy prevailed: in society, the social virtues appropriate to and adapted to feudalism had declined, and conditions had deteriorated to the depths of immorality. Such were the sixth and fifth centuries. Born into this age of disorder, and in the midst of such anarchic and immoral circumstances, Confucius' hope was to re-establish conditions of good government and morality, with the platform of his ideal

—a return to the spirit of the Duke of Chou, the great statesman at the time of the foundation of the kingdom of Chou.

2 *Feudalism and Clan Kinship in the Chou Period*

The later part of the Ch'un-ch'iu period has hitherto been treated as the age which witnessed the breakdown of feudalism. Here the word 'feudalism' has been adopted from its usage in Chinese, as a term for distinguishing the system in question from the later district and prefectural organization: however, in a more general sense, it bears essentially no relation to the modern concept of the word, constituted with the western feudalism of the Middle Ages as the model, and its present-day usage as a term in legal, social and economic history. For a more profound understanding of the spirit of Confucius' times, we should once and for all reject this word 'feudalism' in this usage as a conventional Chinese term, and with an entirely objective and unbiased attitude, enquire whether the administrative and social organization of the Chou period does in fact merit the predication of the term feudalism in its use in the general historical fields enumerated above. Only after a full analysis of the so-called feudalism of the Chou dynasty, in the light of social and economic history, shall we be in a position to recognize the significance in social history of the latter part of the Ch'un-ch'iu period, as being that of the breakdown of the system.

I have already stated that the Chou court divided and distributed its territories to its feudatories, who were to rule on a hereditary basis. Problems which should be examined in the first place concern the precise relation between these feudatories and the royal house, and the prerogatives accorded by the royal house to the

17

feudatories. Secondly, we should enquire into the procedure formulated for relations between the feudatory and the royal house.

There is by no means any rich store of source material on which we can draw for the history of the Chou period. However, material for legal history which refers to the so-called feudal system of the Chou period has been discovered in the considerable number of inscribed bronzes, cast for the purposes of ancestor worship, and to serve as a memorial of honours received from the royal house. These often quote in detail from the text of the documents of appointment bestowed on the feudatory or the high official by the royal house on the occasion of the former's visit to court. Such inscribed bronzes date from the 'Western Chou' period —especially the later part of the period, the ninth and the early part of the eighth centuries B.C.—at the time when Chou still preserved her holy capital at Tsung-chou (with its sanctum in the ancestral temple of the royal house), in the neighbourhood of Ch'ang-an in western Shensi. Such bronze inscriptions are vital material for the study of Chou history; the phrases of the documents of appointment quoted in them, with the detailed records of the ceremonial in connection with the grant of such documents, are specially important sources, and as documents for legal history, they have no equal.

These are supported by such works as the chapters of the 'Book of Documents', in which are collected the exhortations of the Duke of Chou, the great statesman at the time of the first foundation of Chou, and the formalistic poems, called 'Ya', of the 'Book of Odes', thought to be a product of the latter part of the Western Chou period. Further, as we enter the Ch'un-ch'iu period, there are many records in the 'Tso Commentary' and the 'State Discourses' (historical tales of the period), which reveal the breakdown of this so-called feudal system. A synthesis of the evidence from such materials enables to some extent the reconstruction, above all in its legal aspects, of the so-called feudalism of the Chou period.

According to the records of the documents of appointment quoted in the bronze inscriptions, and the poems of the latter part of the period in question, the first and prime duty of a feudatory was attendance at a general congress, called 'the king's meet', which was convened on occasions of the accession of a new monarch, and also at certain fixed times in the year. On such visits, they appear to have presented tribute to the king in the form of the specialities of their local produce, and to have sworn the vassal's oath of loyalty. In addition, in times of peace, they sent coolie labour for engineering works on the defences of the royal city, or the state borders; they supplied food and accommodation and all conveniences to royal legates in peacetime, and to units of the royal troops in wartime when either passed through their territory. A further obligation consisted in the equipping of their own unit, at the command of the ruler, and participation in any joint campaign.

The feudatories further distributed their territory held in fief from the royal house among retainers of the rank of minister, senior officer, and knight, and these retainers owed the same obligations of labour and military service to the feudatories as the latter paid to the royal house.

In the ceremony of enfeoffment when the Chou royal house first distributed its territory among the feudatories, and again when a feudatory brought tribute to court, a bow and arrows, or a chariot, or clothing, in token of land or some other bounty, were handed by the king to the feudatory, and a proclamation in the form of the document of appointment was read, which both lauded a feudatory's ancestors, or the present feudatory in point of his services on behalf of the royal house, and enjoined him to serve the royal house faithfully in the future. In return for this, the feudatory as a pledge of his good faith, presented a jade vessel, and swore to serve the royal house with unswerving loyalty. This ceremony was conducted with all due pomp and solemnity in the imperial palace. There was a similar ritual governing relations between feudatory and retainer. Now this ritual of the document of appointment in which the retainer swears his service in return for the benefactions of the royal house, or the feudatory, and this relationship between king and feudatory, or feudatory and retainer, is very similar to the ceremony of appointment contracted between landlord and retainer in mediaeval times in the west, which is based on the latter's loyal vow to guarantee his service in return for his lord's benefactions.

This superficial similarity merits a more searching enquiry. As has already been stated, the relationship which bound the Chou royal house to its feudatories, and them to their retainers, bears a close similarity to the feudal relationship in mediaeval times between landlord and retainer, in which, in return for the grant of territory, the retainer swore to his lord loyal service which was primarily of a military nature. However, in spite of the similarity of the legal relationship of the bond between lord and subject, a wider view, incorporating a general comparison of the social conditions of the Chou period, and of the Middle Ages in the west, reveals large points of divergence: it would be more proper to regard each as individually conditioned by a differing social framework.

The first point to which attention must be given is the relationship between lord and retainer; this was not a simple agreement between individual lord and retainer, but was rather a bond which was formed between the families to which each party belonged. Especially was this the case with the larger part of the powerful feudatories of the Chou period, for from the son of the Chou ruler down, all belonged to the same clan—that which bore the surname Chi. There was a feudal relationship between king and feudatory based on the oath of loyalty in return for the king's benefactions, but the bond between king and feudatory was not cemented by this alone: king and feudatory were members of the same clan, and there was the additional bond deriving from the relation of the main clan and its branches. The feudatories were all bound as branch clans to the main clan, the Chou royal court, and it was in virtue of this relation based on kinship that Chou controlled her territories distributed in fief. This bond of kinship in the Chou age, between branch families descended from a common ancestor with the main family—the latter maintaining the temple where celebrations in honour of the common ancestor were held, and seeing to the continuation of such celebrations—was a relation which consisted in the service of participation in common worship at the central temple of the ancestor's spirit: a clan of this nature, then, should be regarded as a group which offered joint and common worship. The Chou royal court and the feudatories, descended from the same family stock, assembled as members of a joint community formed for purposes of offering religious celebrations, and while jointly possessing the privilege of enjoying the favours of the spirit of the common ancestor, at the same time incurred in return the duty of offering sacrifice and contributing to the celebrations,

The Chou house, as being the centre of the clan, and the guardian of the temple of the ancestor's spirit, received the service of the clan members paid to the superintendent of the celebrations, and held the privilege of commanding such service. In the relationship binding the Chou court with its feudal kingdoms, this element of clan kinship, rather than any feudal connection, should be regarded as the stronger.

However, the bond between the Chou royal house and families of different stock—i.e. families possessing a different surname—was not of the same nature. Further, it is evident that a great many of the feudatories' retainers came of unrelated families, and there is thus a problem in the nature of the relationship between a lord and his retainer, when the two came from unrelated clans. Here, perhaps, the feudal relationship had stronger force than in the former instance; yet, there existed a further method of linking them, in spite of their alien lineage, as members of a joint religious body. This method, similar to the relation of clan kinship, lay in the joint religious bodies formed for the worship of the local spirits of the land, called 'she-shen' in ancient China, and it was from this origin that there grew the city-state communities of which I shall next write.

3 The Formation of City-state Communities

I wish now, with special reference to Lu, the state to which Confucius belonged, to trace the process of the formation of city-state communities during the Chou dynasty. For this end, we must go back about 450 years from the middle of the sixth century, and the birth date of Confucius, to the early times of the foundation of the Chou realm. The kingdom of Yin, with its seat at Anyang (in Honan province), controlled the plain of northern China, and in the world of the east at the time, it appears to have been the sole community with any claim to culture. (The discovery of the remains of the Yin capital has in recent times attracted world-wide attention among archaeologists). Based on Shensi, far to the west, was the tribe of Chou, which had adopted the culture of Yin, and for a comparatively long period had been tributary. On the accession to the Chou throne of King Wen, whose qualities were such that he was revered as a saint, the tribe subdued its neighbours, who were of different stock, and rapidly gaining power, took the hegemony of the district. King Wen's successor, Wu, snatched the opportunity offered by the gross mis-government of the Yin Emperor Chou, and advancing eastwards, in one coup sacked the capital, destroyed the Yin kingdom, and founded the royal court of Chou. However, on the death of King Wu not long afterwards, the Yin peoples, who had been watching for such an opening, revolted and plotted to re-establish their kingdom, and it was the Duke of Chou, worshipped in Lu as the state founder who, in the capacity of uncle, and Regent to the young King Ch'eng, helped in quelling this rebellion.

The Duke of Chou took personal command of the punitive force sent against the insurgents, who with the Yin peoples, included the commonly called 'eastern barbarian' tribes living in the area bounded by the Shantung peninsula and the River Huai, who were culturally and racially related to the Yin people. The insurgents were harried as far as the distant shore of the Shantung peninsula, and after their armies had been completely liquidated, the Duke of Chou chose Lo-yang as the site for the founding of a new administrative capital. Here, exactly half-way between the old centre of the Yin people, and the original Chou stronghold, he built a base for the government of the central plain.

Residing here, and searching for a solution to the problem of controlling the Yin tribes and the aliens of the eastern areas, he hit upon a plan which might well be termed the national policy of the Chou kingdom: his aim was the creation of a single new civilization, which would reconcile the Chou and the Yin peoples.

The Duke of Chou was a great philosopher as well as a statesman; he severely censured the Yin way of life—for he had not been captivated by its strong faith in sorcery, and its mollifying and sensuous pleasures in wine and the chase. It would be fair to say that the Duke of Chou was the first to perceive the sprouts of religion, morality and learning amidst the magic arts practised in the east, and to discover and to nourish the light of reason among the senses of man. The general belief, firmly held by the people of the Chou dynasty, and especially by those of Lu, the state of Confucius, was that the Duke of Chou created the system of ritual and music of the dynasty, and that he founded the whole of the Chou civilization—with its individual administrative organization, its social system, its code of morality and its arts.

Perhaps with the aim of putting into effect the basic measures which he had instituted for controlling the alien tribes of the eastern area, the Duke of Chou despatched his eldest son, named Po Ch'in, to what is now the prefecture of Ch'ü-fou, in Shantung, in the territory of the alien tribes of the east, and planned to found a Chou colony there. Such was the origin of the state of Lu, which revered the Duke of Chou as its culture hero.

Tradition records that when Po Ch'in, the Duke of Lu, departed for this new outpost, he received a formal document of appointment from the Chou royal house, together with various gifts from the court. First there was the large ceremonial carriage in which the Duke of Lu must ride on the occasion of his visits to the Chou court, and the standard which was flown from it; then the jewel handed down from the kingdom of Hsia, and finally the present of a great bow, said to have been originally the possession of a feudatory of ancient times named Feng Fu. The first three items of this list, used at times of attendance at religious celebrations, served to distinguish the rank of the Duke of Lu at court gatherings. The final gift, the bow, was a symbol of the military authority invested in one who defended a community encompassed by alien tribes, and who had subdued enemies offering resistance to the Chou house. In 501 B.C. (when Confucius was 52), Yang Hu, the steward of the Chi clan, one of the ministerial families of Lu, who had built himself a position of unprecedented power by his revolutionary methods, fell from influence and made good his escape to Ch'i, taking with him this jewel and bow. This latter action caused a great uproar in Lu, for up to the time of Confucius, the jewel and the great bow had been carefully preserved in the state treasury as the hereditary national treasure of the kingdom. Yang Hu's appropriation of these revered ancestral possessions appears to have been viewed as a dire calamity, and the returning of the heirlooms to Lu is recorded in the account of the chronicle 'Ch'un-ch'iu' under the date of the following year. To judge from these events, there existed at least in the time of Confucius, a Lu tradition concerning the foundation which contained reference to the grant of these treasures, as well as to various other privileges.

According to this tradition, apart from the treasures already mentioned, six tribes which were of the same stock as the Yin people, the Tiao, Hsü, Hsiao, So, Chang-shao, and Wei-shao, were also given over to

25

the Duke of Lu, and each tribe was ordered to set up and constitute a central clan and, bringing along with it its branch clans, to leave Lo-yang, and to migrate to Ch'ü-fou, under the orders and in the company of the Duke of Lu. According to this tradition then, the Duke of Lu, when he first went to his command in the new territory, took with him these six tribes who had prior to that been concentrated in the area of Lo-yang, the new Chou capital. Although a people defeated in war, the tradition that these tribes were allowed to set up a centre clan, and retained control over their branch families reveals that at least this section of the Yin people retained their clan organization intact, and were placed under the jurisdiction of the Duke of Lu as complete clan entities.

Thus, when the Duke of Lu set out from Lo-yang, he was already leading these six clans of the Yin population: in addition, in the territory of Ch'ü-fou where he established his capital, there already resided the aboriginals of the state of Yen, who had connections with the Yin people, and taking part in the earlier revolt against the new conqueror, had been subjugated by the Duke of Chou. Further, within the boundaries of the realm of Lu, there resided another alien people by the name of the Feng; these lived both on the banks of the River Chi, the course of which made a great arc through Lu's western sector, and also under the slopes of Mount Tung-meng in the east.

The Duke of Lu's policy in controlling all these alien tribes was founded on the aim to unite them with the Chou people with the clan as the unit. The clan was a celebratory community united by a common religious festival in honour of the ancestor, who was worshipped as the ancestor spirit of the clan: it was ruled by the centre family which watched over the ancestral temple.

However, in accordance with the proverb that a deity would not accept the offerings and services of men not of the same blood, it was held that the deity of the clan would not allow participation in his celebrations to alien clans, or to those other than his blood descendants. Thus the alien clans dwelling in Ch'ü-fou were obliged to search for a deity to whom they could offer joint celebrations. Such a deity was found in the spirit of the soil of the newly founded Ch'ü-fou, and the spirit of the grains which it grew—called in China the 'spirit of the land and grain'. At the foundation of the new capital, the first buildings to be erected were an ancestral temple, for celebrations in honour of the Duke of Chou, side by side with a sacrificial altar for service to the gods of the soil and of the crops. Around these central structures was built the palace of the Duke of Lu, this in turn being surrounded with a fortifying wall.

About two-fifths of a kilometre to the north-east of the present Ch'ü-fou there is a plateau about 450 metres square, which is thought to have been the site of the palace of the king of the area of Lu in Han times. Now since the words 'Ch'ü-fou' mean 'indented hill', the present-day terrace might well be the eminence from which the ancient capital of Ch'ü-fou took its name, and it would be this plateau which would be taken as the centre of the building area when Po Ch'in, the Duke of Lu, founded the ancestral temple, the shrine of the soil and crops, and the Imperial Palace. The district of Ch'ü-fou was said to have been the site of the capital of the Emperor Shao Hao, a ruler of the mythological period, and it may well be that the earlier aboriginal inhabitants lived on the summit of this plateau, and here, too, worshipped Shao Hao as their ancestor, who might thus be regarded as the spirit of the soil of the old Ch'ü-fou. The spirits of the soil and the crops of the newly founded capital on the site, formed from tribes of differing origin can be presumed to have had some connection with the local spirit of the earlier inhabitants, and the latter would have been incorporated as one of the deities to whom worship was to be offered.

Of course, for the members of the Chi clan, that is for those related to the Chou house, as well as for the Duke of Lu himself, the most important deity would be that worshipped in the ancestral temple, as a deity common to the entire clan, and celebrations in his honour would be the most important ceremonies of the kingdom. This being so, as in this age government and religious celebration were not regarded as two quite distinct functions, the Duke of Lu more than any other in the state had the competency to become the priest in charge of the celebrations at the ancestral temple. However, with the title of chief priest of the spirits of the soil and crops, he appears not so much as the head of the ancestral temple, but the priest in charge of the new local cult.

When the Duke of Lu moved to his kingdom, the number of the members of the same clan as he who accompanied him was extremely small. Since the great majority of the population of Lu comprised the six tribes of the Yin placed under the Duke's jurisdiction, together with the earlier inhabitants of the area—the people of the old kingdom of Yen, and the Feng— celebrations in honour of the spirits of the soil and crops were viewed as having much the greater significance for the territorial community which comprised the Lu kingdom. This phenomenon was not confined only to Lu: Wei, Ts'ao, and Tsin, and, in fact, the other communities of Chou stock newly settled in the plain of northern China were all in similar circumstances. The feudatories in charge of these communities all took the title 'chief priest of the altar of the soil and crops' and the practice arose of using the term 'altar of the soil and crops' as synonymous with the word 'state'.

Another fact to which attention should be drawn is that this new territorial community of Lu, drawn together with the celebrations in honour of the spirit of the land and crops as the binding thong, did not have the form of what we are now accustomed to style a state; it did not possess a clearly defined and extensive territory; it had no quantity of urban centres and agricultural villages; it amounted, in fact, to no more than a city-state—as the word indicates, a city surrounded by a small scale wall about one li, or three miles, square. In Chou times, the original significance of the word kingdom was precisely this—the territory within the defensive walls of the metropolis—and the term 'citizen' meant the townspeople residing within the confines of this wall. In conversation with rulers of other states, the Duke of Lu would humbly refer to his own kingdom as 'my small, mean town', and would style states other than his own in honourific terms as 'large cities'. Such was the diplomatic protocol of the age—and it helps to indicate the city-state origin of the various kingdoms of the Chou dynasty.

The process of the formation of the city-state in China hardly differs from that of the Greek and Roman city-state. A survey of the known world of ancient times reveals the surprising phenomenon that from Greece and Rome, and the other Mediterranean kingdoms, Egypt and Mesopotamia, to India, and again eastwards to the several kingdoms of Chou China—all the kingdoms of ancient civilization, although their cultures had their own distinctive features, in social organization were essentially of the city-state type.

In this environment, where the functions of church and state, that is, where state religion and government were inseparably intertwined, when many component clans bound by blood ties were united to form a single community bound by a territorial connection, it would be essential that such a community in the course of its development should pass through the phase of the city-state format. The city-state is, in fact, a stage in the transitional process from a community based on blood relationship to that based on territorial ownership. I believe that it would give a better understanding of its significance in world history to regard the social organization of the Chou dynasty of the sixth and fifth centuries B.C. not as a kind of feudalism, nor (the more restricted term) as ancient feudalism, nor even proto-feudalism, but as another form of the universal city-state structure of the ancient world. Let us now consider the Ch'un-ch'iu period from this latter standpoint.

4 Government by the Aristocracy in the City-state

I have defined the city-state of ancient China as a joint sacrificial community based on the clan as the unit. But apart from this, there is another important aspect of the ancient Chinese city-state; differing from the early Japanese settlements, it possessed a wall by which its limits were enclosed. It seems thus to have been a community assembled with the aim of joint defence against external foes, and should be viewed as a grouping of clans for purposes both of religious cele-bration and defence. When the politicians of the Ch'un-ch'iu city-states said that 'the important affairs of the state concern religious celebration and defence', they were conscious of this dual purpose of the community.

As the economic structure of Ch'un-ch'iu China was founded on agriculture as the major industry, class differentiation was closely bound up with possession of land. But at this period, the term 'land' was not under-

30

stood in the abstract, and there was no conception of the ideas of possession or usufruct. The land was thought of objectively, together with the ideas of possession and usufruct, as being one with the people who resided on, and worked it. When the Chou house succeeded to the Yin empire and unified the realm, the people of Chou were convinced that they had been presented by Heaven with the gift of the land and the people of China: and when the King of Chou distributed the land in fief to the feudatories, he did so in the firm belief that he was dividing among them the land and the peoples granted by Heaven.

At the time of the foundation of the Chou kingdom, the fertile plain of north China was not yet fully opened up, and there remained a wide stretch of untilled land. Hence, among the rewards for military exploits received by the generals of the victorious armies at the time of the Chou conquest, the most vital was not the land itself so much as the inhabitants living on, and working it. An excellent example is to be found in the six clans of the defeated Yin people given over to the Duke of Lu at the time of his appointment to Ch'ü-fou. There are many of the 'documents of appointment' given at the time of enfeoffment in the beginning of the Chou regime, which mention in detail the number of households, or of individuals of the fief in question, and examples of the grant of clans, as in the case of the Duke of Lu, are quite numerous. The clan then was the unit from which the city-state of early Chou was composed, and the clan possessed authority over the land which was assigned to it, and the farmers who worked such lands.

The land granted to these clans was called a 'vassa-lage'. The Chinese term for this is a combination of two characters, the first of which is used in loan for a homonym meaning 'to collect', and thus signifies the right to harvest the fruits, of plant or tree, and the grains produced by the land: the second character denotes a settlement varying in size from ten to a thousand households or families. The method of calculating the area of land in the Ch'un-ch'iu period was not to reckon in terms of the total area, but in terms of such 'vassalages' or estates. A settlement with a certain holding of land with its attached farming population was regarded as an indivisible whole. It had no proprietory rights of its own, but was granted by the state the privilege of retaining the profits accruing from its several settlements. However, only the usufruct of the 'vassalage' was bestowed on the clan by the feudatory; the state was very careful to retain the proprietory rights to the land.

From the middle of the Ch'un-ch'iu period onwards, and especially in its closing years, the sixth and fifth centuries B.C., the clan gradually became separated into more branch families, and on occasions when the family head was forced to flee the realm by reason of an incident such as a political crisis, his family estate was not returned directly into the power of the state, but passed to another member of the same clan. This was the customary procedure, at least, in the state of Lu. But examples are not lacking of cases in which the member of the clan who fled the state continued to control the estate and to receive its revenues as before—though such action was censured as grossly illegal and as a threat to the existence of the state.

The greatest right of the state, that to the ownership of land, gradually came to be titular only; and in contrast to this trend, the tendency of the clan towards gaining proprietory rights became manifest—as in the case of the redistribution of the holdings of members of the clan who had fled the state, where the practice grew of returning such holdings not to the state but to the clan. Thus in the sphere of agricultural land, the clan by degrees encroached on the proprietory rights of the city-state: and in politics also, the actual control of the government of the city-state passed from the hands of the prince, in the person of the feudatory, to those of a representative of a powerful clan. As an example of such a transition of the seat of power, I shall trace the changes in governmental administration in the state of Lu.

The location of governmental authority within the city-state is revealed most plainly by a study of the military control over its armed forces. The army units entrusted with the defence of the state were under the direct authority of the Duke of Lu. They consisted of the members of the communities which had come together for defence and sacrificial purposes, drawn both from the state capital, and from the villagers living in the suburbs and surrounding country. The outlying areas were divided for this purpose into two sections, the left and right (that is, East and West), called districts, from each of which one troop was levied, and it was to a force composed of these two troops that the defence of the realm was entrusted. The commander, his second in command, and an officer given the title of 'Knight of the District' (whose duty was to preside over the important banquet of his District, as the head of his local religious community) were, next to the Duke, the most important officials in the state of Lu.

Inter-state warfare, and also any large-scale inter-necine strife in the Ch'un-ch'iu period was fought from chariots. Troops rode in four-horse chariots, were equipped with armour and helmet, and carried the weapons of the knight—the bow and arrow and the halberd. The fighting power of each troop was reckoned not in terms of the number of soldiers, but the number of horse-drawn chariots which it could furnish. The armed knights who rode in these chariots were of the lowest rank of the noble classes; also called 'officers', they were grouped in units of a hundred or a thousand, and the commanders of such detachments were classed as senior officers, and held a rank above that of the plain knight, but inferior to that of the district officer. It is said that when such senior officers were questioned about the age of their sons, their customary reply was, if the child were adult, 'he is now of an age to drive a chariot', and if still a minor, 'he is not yet old enough to drive a chariot'. Such a convention shows that the most prized privilege of the noble classes in the Chou dynasty (divided as they were into the ranks of District Commissioner, Senior Officer, and Knight), was that of riding in a war-chariot, and of being called upon in the case of war. The common people and, a stage below them, the slave classes, were not entitled to ride in a war-chariot.

In Lu, a community drawn together with the aim of joint religious celebrations and joint military undertakings, the three ranks of District Commissioner, Senior Officer and Knight—the militarily privileged classes in that they had exclusive responsibility for the defence of Lu—preserved a distinction of rank also in the religious affairs of the state, in which they only possessed rights of participation, and from which the common people were rigorously excluded. As government and religion were not regarded as two spheres to be kept distinct, and as court assemblies, which had great significance for administration, were held in the temple of the feudatory's ancestor, and were convened as an appendage, as it were, to the religious festival in honour of the state-founder, the commissioner, officer

34

and knight classes who had the right of attendance at such ceremonies, possessed a special privilege in the political sphere again distinct from and above that of the common people. Thus both politically as well as militarily they formed the noble classes.

There is a sentence describing the range of applicability of common law in Lu—'The ritual does not extend down to the common people; the punishment of the law does not reach up as far as the Senior Officer'. In the first place then, as the plebs was prohibited from taking part in the religious ceremonies of the state, it was consequently completely unable to share in the administration of the state. The religion and the government of the city-state were fields completely closed to the general people, and open only to the class of the knights, and those above them, who had the right, in time of war, of wearing armour and helmet, of carrying halberd and bow, and of riding in a war chariot. In the 'courts'—the conventions held in a square outside the gates of the Duke of Lu's Palace—the right of taking a seat, and of stating an opinion was limited to the class of knights and those superior to them. The noble classes then, as opposed to the general mass, comprised the knights and those above them. (There is, however, a considerable problem as yet not clarified, concerning the exact status of the lowest entity of the noble classes, the knights themselves).

In the second place, the statement that 'the punishment of the law does not extend as far as the Senior Officers' should be interpreted as implying that there was no punishment by means of the laws of the realm for the transgressions of persons of the rank of District Commissioner, or Senior Officer: this statement, however, requires further clarification. In a city-state formed, as in the case of Lu, with the clan as the unit,

35

the internal administration of the clan was left to the free management of the clan itself, and thus the interference of the state in matters involving crimes which were the concern purely of the clan was usually avoided. Only an incident arising between members of different clans became a matter for state arbitration, and such cases also were settled in the 'court' of the state, by discussion between the clan representatives on an appropriate indemnity fixed according to the status of the party concerned, to be paid to the clan to which the plaintiff belonged. However, there were not a few occasions when the clans of each party refused to admit their wrongdoing, or when, the influence of both being almost equal, unable to come to a settlement, they resorted to arms in an attempt to gain revenge. At all events, general penalties were not applied to persons of the rank of District Commissioner and Senior Officer, who were, after all, the most important members of the chief clans from which the state of Lu was formed. In this matter again, the knight was of doubtful category: there were some instances of the application of penalties to persons of this status, but, with the passage of time, and the gradual growth and expansion of the state of Lu, there arose corresponding changes in the influence of the clans which made up the original kingdom, and there would be instances of a weakened person of Senior Officer status losing the right of a voice in the 'court' convention, and of a knight whose extraction was from a clan not possessing the right of speech, and outside the group of early founder clans. In short, the class of knights contained members of a motley extraction, and it would be possible for them, in view of this lack of uniformity to be liable to punishment under the common law. In general terms, then, the government of Lu was aristocratic, since only the three ranks of

36

District Commissioner, Senior Officer, and Knight had the privilege of participation.

5 Aristocratic Oligarchy in Lu

The posts of general of the army, and of premier (these being the most important functions of the District Commissioner), gradually became hereditary to the 'Three Huan'—the three families, the Meng-sun, the Shu-sun, and the Chi-sun, descended from an earlier ruler, Duke Huan. The most influential of the three was the Chi-sun (which is also named simply the Chi): from the middle of the Ch'un-ch'iu period onwards, they manipulated the prince of Lu completely as a puppet, and ran the administration of the state as if it were their own family affair.

The war chariots and the armour and so on used to equip the two troops recruited from the districts of the Lu suburbs, were the property of the state: the two troops were in fact state forces. But the Chi-sun, and the other two members of the 'Three Huan', as the commanders of these forces, as the headmen of the Districts, and again as the superintending ministers of the 'court' conventions, were, as it were, the repositories of public authority; alongside this authority, they placed their own private privileges and thus, apart from the public forces which they controlled by virtue of their appointment from the state of Lu, they also kept private troops under their own personal jurisdiction.

The 'Three Huan' were also members of the village communities which formed the basis of the military organization of Lu. As such, they were in theory knights who held the register of the community, and were no more than the heads of the knights. However, at the same time, the 'Three Huan' had been granted vast estates by the state: that of the Chi lay seventy-five

37

kilometres to the south-east of Ch'ü-fou, and was called Pi; that of the Shu-sun was called Hou, and lay sixty kilometres to the north-west, and that of the Meng-sun, twenty-two kilometres to the north-west was called Ch'eng. Round each of these, solid defensive walls had been built, and each family had levied a great force of private troops, in its concern for the protection of its territories. Such private forces were recruited, in the main, from the descendants of fallen noble families, from the knightly families of the city, and from the sons of the agricultural classes. Every recruit, in accordance with the practice of the day, as a token of his fitness for service, would offer a pheasant—a symbol of loyalty—to his new lord, and it was in this way that the bond between lord and retainer was cemented. In contrast to the public officials in the service of the Duke of Lu, these were private retainers, in the service of a District Commissioner or Senior Officer—himself one of the state's public servants. With the continued increase of authority, and widening of the territory controlled by the 'Three Huan', and the other powerful families, the number of these private retainers gradually grew larger.

The prince of Lu and the noble families were bound together as members of either the main, or a branch family of the same clan. As the original social organization built on the unity of religion and administration fell to pieces, and the authority of the traditional religion waned, there was a natural weakening of the bond which tied the Duke of Lu and the 'Three Huan'. Consequently, from the middle of the Ch'un-ch'iu period, incidents such as the changing, the expulsion, or the murder of a prince at the hands of the powerful noble families became remarkably frequent. The authority of the Lu monarchy, built on the theory of the system of kinship, gradually withered and became ineffective.

The relationship between the powerful families of Lu, such as the 'Three Huan' and their private retainers was an individual one: it had nothing to do with either the clan or the family. The retainer swore personal fidelity to the 'Three Huan', and in return, his lord guaranteed immunity from state responsibilities, such as forced labour, and granted special favours, in the form of plots of land, and so on. The bond between the 'Three Huan' and their private retainers was entirely individual, and was based on the mutual relationship of protection on the part of the lord, and allegiance on the part of his retainer. It is this relation of lord with retainer which should, on inspection, be termed feudal. In the China of the middle Ch'un-ch'iu period, within the various city-states organized on a principle of kinship, the various powerful families at the basis of whose structure stood this feudal relation, gradually began to emerge and ultimately gave indications that they would supplant the lord of the state. The oligarchic control of the influential families within the state was already established, and the social structure of China was on the point of changing from the polity of city-state to that of feudalism.

To take a particular example: in Lu, eleven years before the birth of Confucius, Chi Wu-tzu of the Chi-sun family, the most influential of the 'Three Huan', had, in 562 B.C., proposed the addition of a third troop —thus making a three troop organization of Upper, Centre and Lower Troops—to the existing two troop order of battle, consisting of Upper and Lower Troops. The plan had received the nod of the minister of state Shu-sun Mu-tzu, and had been put into force. It was the aim of this proposal to allocate one of these troops to each of the 'Three Huan' families, and to transform the forces of the state into an entirely private army, under the orders of the three families. As a first move, all war chariots belonging to the state were dismantled: then the lord of the Chi family had all the village community knights in his troop swear oaths as Chi retainers and, in an attempt to convert them completely to the status of private and household troops, he secured for them a remission of all state forced labour. The other lords, the chiefs of the Meng and Shu-sun families, only attempted thus to convert half of the forces allotted to them. This policy was furthered by the disbanding of one troop in 537 B.C., in Confucius' fifteenth year, and the allocation of one of the remainder to the Chi family lord, and the division of the other between the Meng and Shu-sun chiefs. Thus, ten years before Confucius' birth, the forces of the state had become in entirety the private armies of the 'Three Huan', and in his fifteenth year, within the 'Three Huan' themselves the influence of the lord of Chi became overwhelmingly predominant, and with the backing of half of the available forces, he was able to embark on the establishment of a completely auto-cratic government.

Confucius was born in a Lu thus controlled by the oligarchy of the three families, to a father who was in the service of the weaker Meng family, and who as a knight had seen distinguished service in frequent engagements. He was the son of a member of the newly arisen military class, in a China where the transition from a society based on kinship to a feudal polity was just taking shape. In such an age, and such an environment, Confucius was no mere child of fortune: rather, he opened up his own individual 'Way'—not that of the recent development of China's social structure, leading from city-state to feudalism, but one which harked back to the city-state system of the golden age. His 'Way' by-passed feudalism, and led to a new bureaucratic organization.

Confucius cannot be said to have been fully conscious that such were the implications of the 'Way' which he advocated: but I believe that the path which he trod was closely parallel.

TWO

THE EARLY DAYS OF CONFUCIUS

1 The Birth of Confucius

Confucius was born in about the winter of 552 B.C. (the twenty-first year of Duke Hsiang of Lu, who was twentieth in line from the founder Po Ch'in), to a father named Shu Ho (or Shu-liang Ho) who was a resident of the village of Tsou. Confucius' correct name was K'ung Ch'iu—that is, Ch'iu of the K'ung family, Ch'iu being, in Chinese parlance, the real name by which an individual would refer to himself, but by which it would not be correct for others to address him. For this latter purpose a special 'style' or alias was used, that of Confucius being Chung-ni. 'Chung' signifies 'the second son' and as it is known that Confucius had an elder brother, and there is a tradition that his parents died while he was yet young, it may perhaps be surmised that he was the younger of two brothers. It is said that Ch'iu was taken as the real name, and Ni adopted as part of his 'style' because a prayer was offered for the gift of his birth to a mountain by the name of Ni-ch'iu—The Muddy Hill—but the truth of this tradition cannot be verified.

I have written that Confucius was born in about the winter of 552 B.C., but there have in fact been many theories offered from early times concerning the date of his birth: again, I have not quoted his mother's name, as this also raises problems, and, finally, the location of Tsou, the village where he was born, cannot be pinpointed with any precision.

The earliest biography of Confucius appears in the

chapter 'The History of the Confucius Family' in the universal history named the 'Historical Records' written by the great historian Ssu-ma Ch'ien—the so-called 'father of Chinese history'—which appeared during the reign of Emperor Wu of the Han Dynasty. (B.C. 140–81). Apart from his excellence as a historian of the first rank, Ssu-ma Ch'ien was a sincere admirer of Confucius' learning and personality, and was the self-appointed disciple for the propagation of Confucius' 'Way' in Han times. Ssu-ma Ch'ien put his whole heart into his writing on Confucius, and the vivid picture of Confucius' misfortunes—the lofty ideal embraced, the end unattained, the wandering from state to state, and encounters with frequent dangers—all move and touch the sympathy of the reader. It might well be argued that of the 130 chapters of the 'Historical Records', this section secures the most remarkable effect.

It is one of the characteristics peculiar to the Chinese that when once someone of genius has constructed a prototype, all are content to follow the mould, and do not easily go beyond its framework. In the sphere of historiography also, it was felt that the 'Historical Records' written by the genius Ssu-ma Ch'ien should be adopted in toto as the model for history, and thus subsequent Chinese historians have all been content merely to model their work on the 'Historical Records', and have not presumed to create any new form of history writing differing to any great extent. In the case of the biography of Confucius, when once Ssu-ma Ch'ien had written his 'History of the Confucius Family', later authors, by and large, were satisfied with a mere copy, and it is not until comparatively recent times that any has attempted to write a life of Confucius from a novel standpoint.

However, between Ssu-ma Ch'ien, who wrote in the

43

first century B.C., and Confucius, who lived in the sixth and fifth, there was a gap of four hundred odd years: however great the writer's historical genius, such a wide interval could not easily be bridged. There is no great difference between the sources available to Ssu-ma Ch'ien and those still extant at the present, and their volume is indeed extremely slight. The first of these is the 'Analects', a collection of the conversations between Confucius and his disciples. This work which records the scattered sayings of Confucius, may well be a pleasing collection of aphorisms, in which the ideas and the faith embraced by Confucius are revealed in their most concise form, but it is, after all, a farrago of un-related chapters, entirely devoid of any order. It gives no detailed information at any point on questions such as the date and place of Confucius' birth, or the nature of his upbringing at the hand of his parents (about whom nothing is recorded), or again the date of his assumption and resignation of office, and his consequent wanderings outside Lu—and all of these points are of the greatest significance for any biographer of Confucius.

To supplement such deficiencies in the 'Analects', there are the 'Ch'un-ch'iu' Classic (i.e. main text), the annalistic chronicle of the state of Lu, to which Confucius is thought to have made his own additions, and the three commentaries which were appended to the original Classic by three later schools of Confucianism—the Kung-yang Commentary, the Ku-liang, and the Tso-shih. The classic text of the Kung-yang tradition has the entry, under the twenty-first year of Duke Hsiang, 'a day in the eleventh month, birth of Confucius', while that of the Ku-liang tradition records 'winter, a day in the tenth month, birth of Confucius'. There are then such variants—records of either the tenth or the eleventh month—even within the traditions of the 'Ch'un-ch'iu' school.

The text of the classic of the Tso Commentary tradition has no entry relating to the birth of Confucius, but the 'History of the Confucius Family' chapter in the 'Historical Records' differs from the two traditions cited above in placing the date of Confucius' birth in the following year, the twenty-second year of Duke Hsiang of Lu. The Tso Commentary itself also adopts this later date. Biographers of Confucius have offered various hypotheses, based on arguments concerning the calendar of the age, to account for the discrepancy between these two records—but as yet have reached no solid conclusion.

The Tso Commentary enters the death of Confucius in the sixteenth year of Duke Ai, as an event of 'the summer, a day in the fourth month'. This record and the fact of Confucius' death in 479 B.C. have hardly ever been doubted by any scholar up to the present. Confucius left the world before the eyes of Tzu Hsia, and many other devoted disciples, and it is most unlikely that the disciples, thinking back to the acts of the lifetime of the Master they revered, would make any mistake in their recollections of the date of his death. This record would no doubt be passed down to the descendants of the initial disciples, and again to their disciples, as the sect of Confucius steadily gained in power. There should be little room for doubt concerning the veracity of the record of Confucius' death in the Ch'un-ch'iu Classic of the Tso Commentary tradition—no matter when, or by which Confucian scholar, it was interpolated in the official chronicle of Lu.

Among the disciples, who were, by and large, younger than their master, and who, again, joined the 'school' during Confucius' later years, there seems to have been

45

no clear and accurate knowledge of the details of the birth, in mean circumstances, or the indistinct first half of his career. The 'Ch'un-ch'iu' is based on the official chronicle of the Lu court, and so invariably records the death, with the date entered precisely, down to details of month and day, of important public officials such as those of the rank of District Commissioner; but there is not a single instance of an entry for the birth of such officials. In the two Commentaries, the usual custom of the Classic is departed from in a single instance—the record of the birth of Confucius. Since there is no reason why this item should have been entered in the original official court chronicle, the entry must have been interpolated at the time of collation work on the text of the 'Ch'un-ch'iu' by some later member of the Confucian school. And further, in that the accuracy of such a subsequent scholar's calculations with regard to the birth of Confucius is highly suspect, the authority of this record must be dismissed as quite weak.

There is a record in the 'Analects' of the words of Confucius, as, near to the end of his days, he looks back over his lifetime. 'At fifteen, my will was set on the Way of study: at thirty, I was firmly established in this Way: at forty, I had no doubts: at fifty, I knew Heaven's will: at sixty, my ears were obedient, and at seventy, I could follow the yearnings of my heart while yet not transgressing the bounds of proper and becoming conduct'. Confucius then lived at least until the age of seventy. If his death is regarded as occurring in 479 B.C. (the sixteenth year of Duke Ai of Lu), a calculation back to the date of his birth; in the version of the two commentaries, would allow a life of seventy-four years, and by the record of the 'Historical Records', of seventy-three years.

By and large, chronological historians are faced with the problem, common to the ancient history of every civilization, of determining an absolute chronology. In the main, no more can be done than to give a date corresponding to a relative chronology, obtained by summing the figures of the years on the throne of the princes—the latter being provisionally assumed to be accurate. There are many points in the calendar of the Ch'un-ch'iu period which are still a matter for dispute among authorities, and in this respect, any date given for the Ch'un-ch'iu period has no more than relative value. It would be pointless then to seek for any strict accuracy in these records of the date of Confucius' birth —born as he was in humble and insignificant circumstances. In the end, until the appearance of any new and cogent evidence, it seems best, for the sake of convenience, to calculate back from the comparatively authentic date of Confucius' death, and record of his age, and from the two notifications of the date of birth, both within the mathematically possible limits given by this calculation, to adopt the tradition of the two commentaries, thus dating his birth in 552 B.C. (Duke Hsiang's twenty-first year), and to reject the date of the 'Historical Records', the grounds for which are not at all distinct. All statements of the age of Confucius below will be calculated on the basis of this conclusion.

One group of materials on which Ssu-ma Ch'ien drew in writing his biography of Confucius consisted of the traditions current in the area of Lu which was Confucius' home. Some of his facts came from a book not unlike the chapter called 'T'an-kung' of the 'Record of Ritual'. Of course, the 'Record of Ritual' of the time of Ssu-ma Ch'ien does not appear to have assumed the form in which we now have it, but Ssu-ma Ch'ien both read and adopted material for his biography from a section similar to the present 'T'an-kung', the date of the compilation of which is generally agreed to be

47

fairly early. Side by side with this, there are sections of the biography which are thought to have been adopted from traditions handed down in the district of Lu. During his round-tour of the China of his days, Ssu-ma Ch'ien touched Lu, and went to pay homage at the ancestral temple of Confucius within the walls of Ch'ü-fou. Wherever his travels took him, it was his practice to gather local oral tradition, so that some of the statements of this chapter of which the provenance is not clear to us, might well have been based on the stories heard from the mouths of the inhabitants of the area of Ch'ü-fou.

The 'Historical Records' say both that Confucius was born of an improper association of his father Shu Ho of Tsou (otherwise named Shu-liang Ho), with a girl of a Yen family, and also that his birth was granted as the result of a prayer to Mount Ni-ch'iu: the 'T'an-kung' section of the 'Record of Ritual' gives his mother's name as Cheng Tsai, and there is no authority other than that of the 'Historical Records' for the Yen family lineage of his mother. Although this latter evidence is late in date, it appears that the descendants of Confucius at the time recorded in his genealogy that his mother was of the Yen family, and was named Cheng Tsai; and until the appearance of any proof to the contrary, we can do no more than accept these records at face value.

The statement that Confucius' mother, the girl of the Yen clan was not the legitimate wife of Shu-liang Ho is more important. Confucius recognizes Shu-liang Ho as his father and so was probably not an illegitimate child, but a son not of the first wife of his father, but of the secondary wife, or concubine. Later Confucian scholars offered various theories in an attempt to kill the non-classical tradition that the Sage was illegitimate, or born to a concubine. Among these was one modelled on the pattern by that period long common in China, that great and illustrious figures such as the sage kings of old were conceived by the touch of the spirit of the gods: hence it must be that the conception of Confucius after the offering of the prayer to Mount Ni-ch'iu, was attributable to the reception by his mother of the spirit of heaven. This is clearly a later enhancement, an attempt to explain away the tradition that Confucius was not born of a lawful relation—for if the birth was the result of a divine visitation of his mother, the story should simply be told thus, and there should be no scope for the origin of the version that he was born of the union between Shu-liang Ho, and the girl of the Yen clan. Ssu-ma Ch'ien the rationalist would never have incorporated intact such a mystic story of an immaculate conception. Perhaps the most correct procedure open to us now, is to retain the two traditions of the 'Historical Records' (that of the birth of an illegal union, and second that of the birth as the result of the offering of prayers to Mount Ni-ch'iu), but to view them as traditions, and to take care to keep them distinct.

2 The Ancestry of Confucius

According to the 'Historical Records', Confucius' ancestors originally migrated from the state of Sung, which lay ninety kilometres to the south-west of Lu. This source further records the name of Confucius' grandfather as Fang-shu Po-hsia. In the 'Shih Pen', 'The Book of Genealogies', which recorded the ancestry of the various kingdoms of the time, ten generations are recorded from the son of Duke Min of Sung, named Fu Fu-ho to Confucius. If this be regarded as correct, then Confucius' ancestors were of an illustrious family, descended from the royal line. Among the names recorded in these ten generations, appear that of Cheng K'ao-fu, the distinguished scholar who studied in the capital of Chou, Lo-yang, who set in order the scores of the old palace music of Sung, and who compiled the twelve chapters of the 'Shang Sung' ('The Hymns of Praise of Shang') section of the 'Book of Odes', and again that of the famous general K'ung Fu-chia, Cheng K'ao-fu's son, who was the commander in chief of the forces of the state of Sung. Although, in the generation of Confucius' grandfather Fang Shu, the family was driven to seek refuge in Lu, his ancestry was nevertheless noble and illustrious.

However, a closer study of this genealogy recorded in the 'Book of Genealogies', reveals that while no fault can be found with the five generations from Duke Min to K'ung Fu-chia and the three from Fang Shu to Confucius, the two generations between them, of Mu Chin-fu, and of Ch'i Fu, appear in no other source except this. Now from about the middle of the Chan-kuo period, there occurred a great rise in popularity in Chinese thought of the theory of the five elements: this postulated a succession of the elements of wood, fire, earth, metal and water, controlling the physical and human world. Thus the first of these dubious generations, that of Mu Chin-fu, which, in the words Mu and Chin includes wood and metal, two of the five elements, may well be a name worked into the genealogy by Confucian scholars some considerable time after the death of Confucius, at some juncture in the Chan-kuo period, when the theory was at the height of its influence. It seems that this fictitious personage was the key point in the genealogy, by which the descent from Fang Shu to Confucius was to be linked with the famous and illustrious K'ung family of the state of Sung. Thus the

50

tradition of Confucius' descent from this noble Sung family does not warrant any great deal of trust.

Tradition records that Confucius, while yet young, was orphaned by the loss first of his father and then of his mother. It is said that he was distressed at the time of the burial of his mother by his inability to discover the whereabouts of the tomb of his father, but enquiries from a woman of the small town of Tsou, by the name of Man Mu, revealed that it lay in a place called Fang, and he was finally able to bury her with her husband. Thus, according to this story, the tomb of Confucius' father, Shu-liang Ho lay not in the town of Tsou, his place of domicile, but in the village of Fang, where Confucius' grandfather had lived and from which he had adopted part of his name. Shu-liang Ho, then, was not a native of Tsou, but had moved there from Fang, which was located about nine kilometres east of the capital of Lu. Whether or not his ancestors were members of the state of Sung is not clear, but at all events, his grandfather and father had moved their family residence from Fang to Tsou, and Confucius himself made a further move to a place in the eastern suburbs of the Lu capital. Now the noble families of the time all regarded as their real place of residence the town in which were located the tombs and the temple in honour of their ancestors: yet Confucius, whose predecessors had moved from town to village, and who himself subsequently moved back to the capital, was said, at the time of his mother's death, not even to have known the whereabouts of his father's tomb. Even though he is said to have prided himself on his descent from an illustrious family of Sung, we see here the extent to which the two generations immediately preceding him had come down in the world to a status hardly worthy of the title of 'noble family'.

There now remain no traces of records referring to Confucius' grandfather, Fang Shu, but two stories are extant in the Tso Commentary which relate the exploits of his father, Shu Ho as a member of the military forces of the state of Lu. The first, recorded under the year 563, gives a glimpse of his valour at the time of the investment of the fort of Pi-yang, which was an important centre along the line of communication between the central plain and the areas to the south of the Yang-tzu, and lay to the west of the prefecture of I in the modern province of Chiangsu. Previous to this, the league of the states of the central plain, with Tsin at their head, had been constantly harried by the raids and inroads to the north by Ch'u, the powerful kingdom said to have grown from alien tribes, and centred on the modern Wu-han area. Since frontal defence against Ch'u was far from easy, the allied states attempted to attract into their camp the newly risen kingdom of Wu, again composed of alien elements, and situated with its capital in the district of the modern Suchou. The policy of the league was to incite Wu to engage with Ch'u, and thus weaken the force of the latter's northern infiltration. Even in such early times, China's well-known policy of playing off the 'barbarians' was put to full use.

Now Pi-yang lay astride an important junction in the line of water communications between on the one hand, the kingdom of Tsin, whose area of influence extended from the south of Shansi to the northern part of Honan, and on the other, Wu, situated in the area south of the Yang-tzu. Tsin convened the allies of the central plain, and inviting the prince of Wu, held an inter-state conference, the aim of which was to draw up a plan of opposition to Ch'u. The outcome of the convention was that, in an attempt to secure this vital line of communication, the small aboriginal state of Pi-yang was to be attacked, and Hsiang Hsü, a famous minister of Sung, one of the allied powers, stationed there. Lu also supplied troops under its prince Duke Hsiang for the allied force. However, this small fortress, which from the point of view of the forces of the league of the central plain seemed hardly worth taking, was in fact so grimly and stoutly defended that the battle for its capture became unexpectedly drawn-out.

An attempt was made to storm the fort in a single action, but it met with no success. During the engagement, the gate of the fortress was suddenly flung open, and the allied warriors, all wishing to distinguish themselves on this international battlefield, vied to be the first to dash in: then the gatekeeper, watching carefully for the moment, slammed the gate home. Confucius' father Shu Ho of Tsou, in the midst of the startled warriors now struggling to escape, was not in the least unmettled, but grasping a wooden bar, prized one of the leaves of the gate from its hinges, and held it up while the allied warriors made good their escape. Thus to wrench open and hold up a gate single-handed must indeed have demanded remarkable strength.

Such a deed of valour would reverberate not only through Lu itself, but through all the allied states. The general of the forces of Lu at the time was the head of the noble clan of Meng-sun, named Meng Hsien-tzu. Also among the warrior-retainers of the Meng clan was one by the name of Ch'in Chin-fu, who, clasping a length of cloth which had been lowered over the side of the fortress walls to test the warriors of the attacking force, twisted it and climbed up the wall. However, the cloth tore, he fell, and for an instant lost consciousness. Soon reviving, he again twisted it and climbed up. When this had happened three times, the defenders on the top of the wall in admiration of his pluck, rolled up the length of cloth and put it away.

It was not so much reckless daring as cool and steadfast courage on the part of Shu-liang Ho which had ensured the escape of his comrades. It was said that Meng Hsien-tzu, the head of the Meng clan, the history of whose house shone with brilliant military exploits, engaged in the service of his family knights whose bravery he especially admired. The valiant action of Confucius' father would not easily slip from men's minds, and there was no doubt some connection between it and the subsequent summons to Confucius to undertake the education of the sons of the clan of Meng-sun.

Confucius' father, his military prowess given full recognition after the incident at Pi-yang, seems thereafter to have been employed by his state for important military missions. Seven years later, in 556 B.C., Lu was raided by her powerful northern neighbour Ch'i, who still remembered the days of her former hegemony of the central plain under her Duke Huan, and throughout the Ch'un-ch'iu period was a menacing and formidable enemy. The attacking force of Ch'i was split into two columns one of which laid siege to Fang, the seat of the illustrious Lu family of Tsang-sun. A relieving force was despatched from the capital, but was afraid to approach too near to the fort. One of the men holding Fang was Confucius' father, who had been given command of a detachment of the defending troops. Taking counsel with the Tsang family, in the case of any untoward turn of events, he had advised that the family head should make good his escape from the beleaguered fort, and so, with an escort of the young stalwarts of the clan, and three hundred knights, he guided the head of the house, Tsang-sun Ho, through the lines of the besieging Ch'i forces. Under cover of night, the party reached the camp of the relieving force from Lu, reported the situation to them, and Shu-liang Ho then immediately retraced his steps, attacked the investing army, and returned to Fang.

To break through the siege lines of an overwhelmingly superior enemy under his very eyes, and to establish contact with the friendly army was a feat demanding great courage: but, on the accomplishment of this mission, to retrace one's steps straightway to the main fort which was under siege and would fall at any moment, demanded an even greater show of valour. Nor was it simply courage that was called for; without a very strong sense of duty, the assignment could never have been successfully accomplished. Confucius' father appears to have been a man with the requisite qualities for the successful accomplishment of such dangerous missions.

The point to note in these two exploits of Confucius' father is that they were not brilliant feats of arms in a victorious battle, such as the capture of the head of the enemy general, or the leading of a column of attacking chariots. Instead, he helped his comrades escape from a locked gate, and escorted his prince from his beleaguered seat to the hands of a relieving army—both actions of an unpretentious nature. Confucius' father in sheer physical strength yielded to no man: his courage was boundless, but was not born of recklessness, but rather of cool discrimination, and a staunch sense of duty. With his calm courage and loyal heart, he was the ideal warrior: in times of peace, also, such a man would be strong of integrity, and firm of will.

It might well be imagined that, in the period of the decay of the city-state system towards the end of the Ch'un-ch'iu era, it was from this soldier father with lofty ideals that Confucius inherited his heroic nature, exemplified in his unbending and unflinching struggle to bolster up the tottering framework of society, and to establish it on the foundation of the ideal system of the 'Way' of the Duke of Chou.

According to the 'Historical Records', Confucius was nine feet six inches tall, a height which seems to have been regarded as quite unusual. The measures of length of the Han dynasty were shorter than those now in use: the height of a normal adult was about seven feet, that of a tall person eight feet: thus a height of nine feet six inches indicated something of a giant. The representative Confucian scholar of the end of the Chan-kuo period, Hsün Tzu says that Confucius was tall, and his disciple Chung Kung was short. Perhaps the source which Ssu-ma Ch'ien employed for these figures was a tradition remaining in the Lu area in Han times, and thus the statement of Confucius' height may well not be entirely accurate. On the other hand, tallness and physical strength in Confucius may easily be explained as a legacy of his famous warrior father.

When Confucius in his later years visited the neighbouring kingdom of Wei, its prince, Duke Ling, requested that he discourse on the arts of war. To this, Confucius replied; 'I have heard something of matters relating to sacrificial and religious vessels, but I have never heard of the affairs of armies and troops', and indignantly left Wei. Yet Duke Ling might well have been forgiven for making his first question one concerning the arts of warfare, when he saw Confucius—the son of an illustrious warrior of Lu, whose imposing physique well befitted his ancestry. Yet though born the son of a warrior, and blessed with a stature appropriate to his birth, Confucius' aim was not, strangely, to rise to fame as a warrior in command of troops, but to come to prominence as a statesman, and to settle the world's plight by means of what he termed 'sacrificial and religious vessels', that is, by a social reformation based on the ceremonial and the music of religion.

3 The Circumstances of Confucius' Youth

Unqualified acceptance as a fact of the lineage of Confucius as a member of a well-known family which traced its ancestry back to a noble clan of Sung, has led to a ready tendency to imagine the circumstances of his life as those of a noble. Biographers, such as the writer Lin Yu-t'ang who has written a new critical life of Confucius, understand him as a noble with refined interests and delicate susceptibilities, his life surrounded with all the elegance of the aristocrat. The adult Confucius regarded nobility—the concept of the 'princely man'—as the ideal of human culture, so that a certain degree of respect, on his part, for the life of the noble cannot be denied. This respect and adulation, however, should be understood as a product of the unfulfilled desires of his youth, when his circumstances were so entirely the opposite of the ease and luxury of the noble's life.

Confucius' father Shu-liang Ho held a rank and salary befitting the status of his family: he was no noble. His reputation and position as a valiant soldier were gained as a result of his outstanding military skill and bravery, and his quick-thinking exploits as a soldier. He was a member not of the hereditary aristocratic class, but of the class of military knights which had risen to prominence in the middle part of the Ch'un-ch'iu period, and the years following, and had been engaged in service by the noble classes, by reason of the military skills they had acquired, gaining their livelihood from such employment.

The noble families, that is the 'princely men', owned vast estates in the farming areas, and fed and clothed themselves on the income derived from them, although at the same time they built villas in the vicinity of the city-states and in normal times resided there. The nobles were townspeople, who lived inside the city walls. In contrast, the common people, called the 'small men'— in virtue of being under the control of the nobles—were the agricultural multitude who lived beyond the city wall, in the 'fields'. When Confucius first took office and was officiating at a service in the Sung ancestral temple in Lu, he is said to have been ridiculed by the inhabitants of Lu, one of whom said, 'Can any son of Tsou really know the ritual?' This term 'son of Tsou' is one of contempt for the son of a military knight living in the country, used by a member of the urban noble classes residing in the Lu capital Ch'ü-fou. For, even though in his later years Shu-liang Ho advanced to the rank of divisional commander, a status merited by his military exploits, he still remained a country parvenu: boorish and uncouth, his life would not contain the refinement and elegance which marked that of the urban noble.

Thus while it is clear that Confucius drew such upstart military class ancestry from his father's side, there is no evidence that his mother came of any illustrious Lu family; she appears in fact to have come from the obscure common people. Furthermore, there is the tradition that the relations between the Yen clan girl and Shu-liang Ho were not those of a properly regulated marriage, and Confucius, born of this union, was quickly separated not only from his father, but also, by her death, from his mother, and became an orphan with none at all on whom he could call. The circumstances of his youth then were not at all in keeping with the usually envisaged favoured life of the noble class; a destitute orphan, he must have suffered the extremes of misery.

The prime minister of the state of Wu, which during the lifetime of Confucius had come to the fore in the affairs of the central plain, and which Lu also, at one stage, recognized as the head of the confederacy, in conversation with Tzu Kung, one of the disciples of Confucius who had become a Lu envoy, had once asked why it was that although his Master was a sage, he had such an extensive knowledge of minor matters. When he heard of this, Confucius turned to Tzu Kung and replied, 'When I was young, I was poor: hence my many abilities in mean matters. Does the princely man possess many such skills? No! Not many.' Earlier, Confucius had also said 'The princely man is not a tool'—and by this he had meant that the princely man, the ideal of the noble, did not and should not practise any special technique so as to qualify himself for some particular calling, but should possess an education of his complete personality, to fit himself for governing those who fulfilled such tasks. This being so, any show of aptitude for, or ability in common matters did not indicate the princely man or the noble; it was deemed something of a defect, which did not at all befit the sage. However, Confucius confessed that he was born into humble and mean circumstances, and that he was obliged to forgo the broad and general upbringing of the noble, having to pay prior attention to the learning of special professional techniques.

The 'Analects' gives no clear indication of these technical skills which Confucius had acquired. Once he said to his disciples, 'What shall I take up? Shall it be driving or archery? I think it shall be driving'. It seems that he could never bring himself to make a special art of the military techniques, of driving a war chariot, or of taking up bow and arrows in a national emergency—arts which an army knight could not afford to neglect: this, too, in spite of his being the son of a knight who had gained wide fame in Lu, was something quite beyond the limits of his way of thought. Broad of frame though he was, and perhaps possessed of the strong arm that went with his size, this valiant knight's son had no desire for achievement as a professional soldier.

According to the 'Historical Records', as a child, Confucius used to amuse himself by playing at arranging three jewels in correct ritual position, and offering them to the gods. Of course, the veracity of this tradition cannot be established, but it seems a very probable story. Though the son of a warrior, he said that in his youth 'When I was fifteen, my heart was set on study'. This is a drastic deviation from the way of life he had inherited, and from the environment to which he had become accustomed: but what motive he had in his choice of the completely alien field of study, and his decision to put his faith in the meagre income which would accrue from the poor life which his choice entailed, is now, unfortunately, incapable of clarification. He says of himself that 'At forty, I had no doubts': during the interval, then, between his initial discovery of a zest for scholarship, and the final establishment of an individual way of thinking, at the age of forty, there may well have been periods of deep anxiety. But he adds that, 'At fifty, I understood the decree of Heaven', by which he indicated that at this age, had materialized the realization that his initial decision to devote his life to study was a task imposed on him by Heaven. According to his mental outlook in later years then, study was a duty enjoined by Heaven. But for

Confucius, the agent was of less moment than the motive: he said of the motives of study, 'Scholars of the old school studied for themselves; those of today do it for others', by which he seems to have meant that the scholars of his own times studied as a means to an end, to display and boast of their scholarship to others; but the old-time scholar—by which he indicated the ideal scholar—made scholarship an end in itself. It might be more true to say of Confucius, not that 'he chose a life of scholarship', but that 'he naturally entered into the way of the scholar'.

4 Confucius' Education

Confucius recollected that at the age of fifteen (in 538 B.C.), he set his mind on the way of study. But the 'Analects' and our other sources say almost nothing on such questions as the person of his teacher, and the nature of the education he received from such a teacher. The following story may be unreliable, in that it may have originated after Confucius' death, after the spread of his fame as a scholar. A noble, one Kung-sun Ch'ao of the state of Wei asked Tzu Kung, one of the more prominent disciples of Confucius, from whom the latter had received his education. In reply, Tzu Kung argued that the old Way of the Chou founders, the sage-kings Wen and Wu, decayed though it might be, had still not entirely disappeared: it still remained among men, of whom the worthy remembered its great points, while the small and mean man recorded its small and minor aspects; each of these was, nevertheless, a part of that Way. This being so, 'Where could our Master go where he could not find the opportunity for study? And what need had he of a regular teacher?' That is to say, Confucius could and did learn from any situation, from any person, and that he had no need of any specially selected teacher to give him regular tuition.

The prevalent custom of the times was that a special and regular teacher, not unlike the modern private tutor, should be appointed for the education of the sons of the noble classes. This being the case, the person who questioned Tzu Kung concerning Confucius' tutor, took it for granted that a scholar of this standing had gained his learning at the feet of some great and famous teacher. To counter this impression, Tzu Kung replied that it was not from any teacher that Confucius learned the Way of King Wen and King Wu: this Way was not something which was written down in the form of a single and systematized body of thinking. Rather was it something which he had picked up and adopted from traditions still extant in the society of his day, and living, in some degree, in every single person.

Giving warning to his disciples, in a statement recorded in a verse of the 'Analects', Confucius says, 'At home, you should be filial: abroad, show respect for your elders: be worthy of trust, and honourable, extend your love to include all mankind, and make a friend of the good. Use what powers and chances that remain after practising these precepts, for the study of the writings'. In other words, only when he is capable of acting in accordance with such canons of behaviour should a disciple read and study the literature—the works in which was recorded the Way of the former kings. Again, he said, 'The Princely Man does not aim to fill his belly, or live in ease; diligent in his actions, circumspect in his speech, he rectifies himself by the model of men who know The Way. Such a man can truly be called a lover of learning'.

The stress then was more on the practice than on the theory of moral action. To those who sought him out as a teacher, he did not so much expound a theory of morals, as offer criticisms of certain conduct already put into effect. In his school, there was no need of assiduous and sustained application to study; he was satisfied with an occasional sounding of his pupils' views. In this aspect, Tzu Kung was correct in arguing that Confucius had no need of a regular tutor: the orphan son of the warrior simply could not have adopted some scholar of repute as his teacher, and received special instruction from him.

During the Ch'un-ch'iu period, it was part of the social organization, in the case of persons of and above the rank of knight, to group five households into a small local association: five of these associations formed a hamlet, four of the latter formed a larger group again, to which was given the name 'clan': five 'clans' formed a village society, five of these an area community, and, finally, five of these areas were organized into the largest such grouping—the 'district'. In origin, these were communities of the general residents of an area formed together on a residence basis, for both religious and military purposes, and each community appointed its elders as teachers, there being administrative machinery for a fixed term of education for all the children in the territory under its care. Schools were set up in the village societies (the groups of five 'clans'), and when Confucius said that at the age of fifteen, his mind was set on study, he meant that he entered a local school of this nature.

Education in these local schools, at the hands of the elders of the community, would consist of a training in religious ceremonial connected with the worship of the deities of the clan, and in the behaviour and etiquette practised in the year-round activities of the community. Social convention of this period demanded the highest

63

respect for the aged; the etiquette of the banquet which was held in association with religious celebrations in honour of the clan deities in country communities such as these 'villages' and 'districts', was committed to writing by the Confucian school as a chapter of the 'Book of Ceremony and Ritual', with the title, 'The ritual of wine-drinking in the local community', and Lu scholars even in Han times practised a ceremonial modelled after it. In the 'district', the basis of the ritual lay in the youth: hence, the elders were invited to sit at the feasts, and asked to recall bygone events told of in the oral traditions of the community. Such, in fact, was one of the aims of the ceremony. The aim of education in the elementary course of study in the district schools, was to teach the young the etiquette of respectful service to their elders, and to give them instruction from their elders in the history of the community—in short, to enable them to grow up into useful adult members of the group.

At the age of fifteen, Confucius would enter such a local primary school, and be taught by his elders what was deemed necessary for him to become a good member of their community. His education stopped short within the narrow limits of the locality, confined as it was to didactic stories handed down through the village's history.

Lu, far removed from the cultural centre of the Honan plain, and lying somewhat out of the way to the east, had hitherto not played any vital role on the stage of the inter-state warfare of China, and, compared with some other states, had lived in comparative peace. But now, it lay in the direct line of assault of the newly risen kingdom of Wu to its south. Again, internally, there was opposition between the Duke of Lu and the noble families, and violent social unrest finally reached the point where the Duke was obliged to flee to the neighbouring state of Ch'i. Such menacing conditions, both external and internal, could not but permeate through to the quiet local districts, and leave their impression on the mind of the young and sensitive Confucius. He seems to have lifted his eyes, and looked out far beyond the narrow confines of the walls of his state, and to have been plunged into deep distress as he beheld the fate of the whole of the people of China.

THREE

CONFUCIUS AND HIS PREDECESSORS

1 Traditionalism

After entering the local school at the age of fifteen, Confucius received, at the hands of the old man of the borough, a training to fit him for a natural performance of ritual and procedure as a member of his district community. He says of himself, 'At thirty, I was established'—by which he meant that at that age, he already felt a firm self-confidence that he could leave the classroom of the village elders, and advance independently and by his own steps on the path of study. Let us first look at his own statements about his attitude to study. He once remarked, 'Even in a hamlet of ten houses, there will always be one whose loyalty and reliability is the like of mine, but there will be none who loves learning as I love it'. Normally so extremely modest, Confucius here speaks with strong self-assurance; his love of learning is clearly so ardent as to be incapable of comparison. The aim of this love of learning was 'to transmit, and not to create: to trust in, and to love antiquity'. Again, 'I am not one of those who possess innate knowledge. I merely love antiquity, and earnestly seek it'. Confucius, then, found the object of his studies not in the hard facts of his own social environment, but far beyond and behind that, in the traditions of antiquity, in other words, in the world as it was pictured in the classics.

After his death, Confucius' disciples recalled their master's attitude to learning in the words, 'The Master spoke the "Odes" and the "Documents" in formal language, and in conducting the ritual, he invariably used formal language'. That is, when reading the 'Odes' and the 'Documents'—the classics of later Confucianism—he did not employ the dialect of his native Lu, but the standard and formal language of Chou; and again, in handling any ceremony, he spoke in the standard pronunciation. He liked above all else to read the 'Odes' and the 'Documents', for in the principal parts of the 'Analects', it is invariably these two works which are quoted in conversations between Confucius and his disciples.

I have said that Confucius used to love to 'read' the 'Odes' and the 'Documents'. This wording perhaps involves an inaccuracy, and it might have been more correct to say loved to recite them. In such recitation, the words were not given their normal everyday accent and intonation, but were mouthed in very solemn tones. The 'Odes' comprised three main sections; first, the libretti, called 'Hymns of Praise', of the music sung to the accompaniment of an orchestra and offered at festivals in honour of the spirits of the august founders of the kingdom of Chou: secondly, the formal songs sung on the occasion of a banquet in honour of state guests at the court of Chou, and lastly, the 'State Airs'— the words of the music offered to the Chou court from the various states of the realm. The 'Odes' contained many verses in praise of the achievements of the ancestor heroes, King Wen, and King Wu, who had overthrown the state of Yin, and had founded the kingdom of Chou. The lines of the 'Odes' consisted of four monosyllabic characters, of which the final character rhymed, and were intoned to the accompaniment of musical instruments. Even when read without such accompaniment, they still retained a very smooth-flowing rhythm, and a character which forced the reciter to vary the modulation of his voice, and intone to himself. These rhyming verses, of such systematized format, even when not set down in writing, were of their nature easily committed to memory.

At the Chou court, there was an orchestral group consisting of a number of blind musicians, whose function it was to give special performances of the 'Odes'. Blind men do, in general, possess the ability to memorise with the greatest facility, and the blind musicians of Chou period China, without either the words or the music, sang the 'Odes' completely from memory. Thus it was by oral transmission alone that the words and music of the 'Odes' were passed on from father to son, and instilled by teacher into pupil. A group of music masters from the special orchestra of the Chou royal household who were the repositories of these traditions, was sent to the court of Lu, a branch clan of the Chou house. It is to be presumed that Confucius, having studied ritual and procedure and the ancient history of the locality in the district elementary school, would presently have gone on to the University in Ch'ü-fou, the Lu metropolis, there to study the 'Odes' under this group of blind court musicians.

It is stated in the 'Analects' that whenever he met a blind man (i.e. a blind musician), even though the latter be younger than he, Confucius invariably gave up his seat, and bowed in deference. Again, on the occasion of a visit by a musician by the name of Master Mien, Confucius pointed out 'the steps are here', at the bottom of the staircase, and as he was stepping up to a seat, he guided him with the words 'the chair is here'. The disciples were astonished at what they thought was the excessive politeness of this interview, and there is a record of their cross-questioning of Confucius on the question whether such procedure was correct or not.

The office of Music Master was hereditary and was treated with some contempt by the noble classes as being filled by commoners. Confucius, however, treated the musician not merely with the respect due to a fellow man, but even with the full polite ceremonial due to a Master.

The text which now bears the title 'The Old Documents' (or, simply 'The Documents'), is a collection of the texts of the proclamations issued to the people by, in the first place, the sage kings Yao, and Shun, then the various emperors of the Hsia and Yin dynasties, and the rulers and first ministers of the Chou kingdom, such as King Wen, King Wu, and the Duke of Chou. It is very probable, however, that the sections of the work treating of the Yin dynasty, and the periods before that time, were not yet completed at the time of Confucius, that there were as yet only the sections containing the admonishings of the Duke of Chou. The 'Documents' was not made up of lines containing four characters, as was the case with the 'Odes': the structure was not based on any determined line length, and the lines were not rhymed. Hence, in comparison with the 'Odes', it was much more difficult both for memorization, and for transmission by oral means only. Quite probably, it was not handed on purely by oral transmission, but was at an early stage committed to writing. The books of the age were not of paper; bamboo, or some other kind of wood, was cut and made into strips, or plates, a number of which was then put and held together by leather thongs, and on which characters were written by the incisions of a stylus. Such documents were clearly inconvenient both to read and to preserve, and consequently, the range of their circulation would be very restricted. Archives would probably only be stored at the offices of the official known as the 'Grand Historian', or the 'Internal Historian' of the Chou royal court, and the several state capitals. It may well be that Confucius learned to read the 'Documents' from this official Archivist at the Lu capital.

Naturally, at the time of Confucius, the works which we now have on ritual, the so-called 'Three Rituals' ('Ceremony and Ritual', 'Record of Ritual' and 'Chou Ritual'), were not yet compiled. His references to 'the ritual', were probably, in the first place, to the official called the Master of the Temple, who was in charge of ancestral festivals and to the traditions concerning procedure in celebration ceremonies, which were preserved in the various offices in Lu and in the households of the different noble families. Confucius would learn of the various rituals and procedures from the officials who presided over the different ceremonies, as is clear from a part of the quotation of the 'Analects' cited above: 'when the Master entered the Great Temple, he asked about every detail, so that some wit was driven to ask, "Can some son of a man of Tsou know the ritual?"—for he always asks about everything when he goes into the temple.' When he first became an official of some standing in Lu, and took a part in the celebrations at the temple of the state ancestors, he asked questions of the assistants of the Master of the Temple, concerning every detail of the procedure, and he was described insultingly as the great ritual scholar-son of a country yokel. It was then from these officials of the Board of Ceremonies that Confucius received training in procedure of this nature.

The young Confucius then, with his ardent love of learning, first studied the ceremonial of the local community with the erudite and well-informed elders of the village school. Then he went on to read the 'Odes' and the 'Documents' with the Music Master, and the Archivist, at the establishment for higher learning in the Lu capital, and also imbibed all manner of traditions concerning the ritual from the Director of Ceremonies. But these achievements did not satisfy him.

About 170 kilometres to the south-east of the capital of Lu, in the present day prefecture of T'an-ch'eng, there lay the state of T'an. In the year 525 B.C., its ruler, who ranked as a viscount, paid a court visit to Lu. At the welcoming banquet usual in the entertainment of visiting foreign princes, Shu-sun Chao-tzu, who was the First Minister of Lu, asked the meaning of the story that in the reign of the emperor of ancient times, Shao Hao, all officers were given titles after the names of birds. In reply, the Viscount of T'an said that the Golden Emperor had given cloud names to his officers, and the Fire Emperor had used terms connected with fire: Kung Kung used water terms, and Ta Hao gave dragon names. Further, since Shao Hao was the ancestor of his own state of T'an, he was in a position to know the reason for this measure: it was that, as at the commencement of his reign, male and female phoenices had flown down from Heaven, he had used the names of birds for official titles in accordance with this good omen. The Viscount had then recited in detail the names of each official, and had completely confounded the dignitaries of Lu.

When he heard of this, Confucius went forthwith to visit the Viscount of T'an at his place of residence in Lu, and learned from him in detail about the events of the reign of Shao Hao. On his return, Confucius declared that the Chou ruler could no longer effectively control his officers, that all traditions concerning these offices were lost in the central states, but still lived in the kingdoms of the barbarians. T'an, although a barbarian state, and unrelated to the Chou house, had preserved the traditions of this early part of China's history.

The formation of a tradition of a succession of five sage emperors, with the Golden Emperor at their head, should be dated to about the middle years of the Chan-kuo period, long after the lifetime of Confucius. The argument of the Viscount of T'an, in his explanation of the differences in official titles at the time of the Five Emperors must then be regarded as an interpolation of Chan-kuo date in the text of the Tso Commentary, in which this account appears. But, considerations of the problem of the detailed content of the Viscount's argument apart, the story of Confucius' questioning a 'barbarian' ruler on the matter of the vestiges of regulations of earlier dynasties, can fairly be regarded as showing the type of man Confucius appeared to be to the people of Lu in the Chan-kuo period.

Thus, whether his conversation be with the lowly Music Master, or with the prince of an alien state, Confucius, regardless of a man's social rank or his nationality, sought for instruction in the way of the sage kings of old. Especially did his admiration tend towards the Duke of Chou, who was believed to be the author of the main sections of the 'Odes' and the 'Documents', and was regarded as the founder of the ritual of the Chou dynasty. Towards the end of his life, lamenting the loss of ardour of his feelings of attachment to the Duke of Chou in the time of his youth, Confucius said, 'Indeed, I am failing badly, for it is a very long time since I saw the Duke of Chou in my dreams'. The subject of the dreams of his youth seems invariably to have been the Duke of Chou.

The past which Confucius admired was, in concrete terms, the classics of the 'Odes', and the 'Documents', and the Ritual, which infused life into these classics. He went a stage further, for from this understanding and admiration of the world of the classics, he passed on to contemplate the eminent Duke of Chou, who had created the world reflected in the classics. This further admiration did not spring simply from any patriotic feeling towards the Duke of Chou as the ancestor of the ducal house of Lu, Confucius' own state. His love of the ritual and music of the Chou court which still lived in his time did not stop short at the recognition of its supreme beauty or essential goodness: rather he understood such goodness and beauty to be the manifestation of the perfect personality of its creator, the Duke of Chou. Confucius' love of antiquity was not merely a treasuring of the civilization of old, a barren antiquarian interest: from his own peculiar standpoint, the civilization of antiquity was viewed all along in close connection with its founder. His reverence for antiquity sprang from his emotional reactions to the beauty of its culture, and was intensified to become an understanding of the personality of its creator. His outlook could be termed classicism, or traditionalism, but one should not be misled by these terms into interpreting his attitude as simply a reverence for the dead culture of the past; his classicism found expression rather in his tremendous respect for the personality of an illustrious man. Humanism, a reverence for humanity, was fundamental in his outlook, as can be gathered from his reaction to the news that the small stables in the court had burnt down: his only question was, 'Was anyone hurt?'—no reference at all to the horses.

Should there arise a conflict between the claims of tradition and humanism, what kind of circumstances would such a conflict create? For classicism, tradition holds the place of absolute authority, to which humanism must of necessity be subordinated. However, in Confucius' classicism, this reverence for humanity, and

73

the authority of tradition both had equally essential parts to play. More fully to understand the significance of this assertion, we must investigate more deeply Confucius' traditionalism: and, to understand it, we must glance back at conditions in the world of thought in the China of the age when Confucius' ideas were beginning to take shape.

2 The Age of Government by Sage Ministers

For the political historian, and also the historian of thought, the clue to the question of how to define the period from 538 (when Confucius, at the age of fifteen, first set his mind on study) to 523 B.C. (when at the age of thirty, he finally began to formulate his own way of thinking)—in fact the formative period of Confucius' thinking—is to be found in the death, in 522 B.C., when Confucius was thirty-one, of Tzu Ch'an, the Prime Minister of the state of Cheng. Cheng was one of the states of the central plain, and the death of its minister, a wise administrator, was an event of deep significance for the impressionable period of Confucius' education.

Together with Tzu Ch'an, whose name, by reason of his wide learning, was known throughout China, should be ranked Yen Ying, scholar and first statesman of Ch'i, the powerful state of the east, on Lu's northern borders, whose name was given to the 'Yen-tzu Ch'un-ch'iu', a treatise on political science. Again, in Tsin, the state which at the time was the head of the confederacy of the states of the plain, there was Shu Hsiang, who, although not actually in office, was yet an influential political adviser. With these wise and worthy administrators each controlling policy in the city-states of the central plain, this is one of the noble points in the political history of ancient China. The age might well be called that of 'worthy ministers'. Tzu Ch'an first occupied a lowly place in the government of Cheng in 554 B.C., two years before Confucius' birth; his death occurred in 522 (when, as said before, Confucius was thirty-one), precisely at the time when Confucius was coming to the realization of his own personal standpoint. The formative period of Confucius coincides exactly with the period of office of this famous minister.

The common characteristic of these three wise administrators, Tzu Ch'an of Cheng, Yen Ying of Ch'i, and Shu Hsiang of Tsin, is that they were all born into comparatively weak noble families. Since the early part of the Ch'un-ch'iu period, frequent internal disorder had occurred in Cheng, over the problem of the succession of the ruler, and the actual control of the kingdom had passed into the power of those noble clans from whom the highest official of the state was selected. The privilege of offering candidates for selection as premier was strictly restricted to the seven branch families, called 'the Seven Mu', descended from Duke Mu of Cheng, and since Tzu Ch'an came of a family not of this select group, his influence was not to be compared with such as the Ssu, or the Liang families, who were eligible to put up candidates for the premiership.

In Ch'i, the first minister was chosen at this time from the flourishing Ts'ui family, the Ch'ing family, and the Ch'en family which had intermarried with the two older families and by degrees had increased its power. The Yen family, of which Yen Tzu came, was of alien stock, residing on the seaboard of the eastern part of Shantung province. This was indeed a lowly and impoverished family. The families in Tsin which controlled the office of the premiership were the six clans (called the 'six officers') Han, Wei, Chao, Fan, Chung-hang, and Chih. Shu Hsiang was born into a ducal clan, by the name of the Yang-she, which traced back its origin to an

75

early Tsin ruler. Families related to the ruling line of Tsin had for long held little power, and at this juncture, were almost on the verge of extinction. Shu Hsiang appears as their last representative, before they sank into complete obscurity.

It may well be asked how it came about that these three scions of weak and lowly families, Tzu Ch'an, Yen Tzu, and Shu Hsiang were able to reach important offices which controlled the government of their respective states. This was an extremely important phenomenon in the history of politics in the Ch'un-ch'iu period, and many kinds of explanation might be offered. I believe, however, that this situation was brought about by the state of equilibrium produced for a time by the social forces at work in the middle years of the Ch'un-ch'iu period. From the start of the Ch'un-ch'iu period, the real authority in the government of the city-states had passed gradually to the powerful noble classes—to the six families in Tsin (the so-called 'six ministers') and in Lu, to the three families called the 'Three Huan'. This was, in fact, a transition towards oligarchy. However, by the time of the middle years of the Ch'un-ch'iu period, between these families of noble birth and in high positions, there had broken out violent struggles for power, and in the course of countless repeated internal uprisings, a great many of these powerful families had suffered total extinction. Among the remaining noble families there had grown an atmosphere in which, in order to alleviate the anxious panic of the common people, and to enhance the chances of a period of internal tranquility, the noble families agreed on the choice of some neutral party for the office of premier: it was hoped that his neutrality in such internecine quarrels would make for a greater degree of stability and continuity in the administration of the state. As candidates for such intermediary functions, it was thought that the most appropriate would be those drawn from old established noble families whose influence had never been very great, and from whose ranks it had not hitherto been the practice to select the premier, yet who still possessed members who combined the qualifications of political acumen with wide general knowledge. The fact that Tzu Ch'an, Yen Tzu, and Shu Hsiang, all of whom came from small and weak families, were nominated to the rank of premier, or some official position akin to it, was a product of this state of equilibrium in the influence of the opposing noble families in each state.

It was in this way then that men like Tzu Ch'an and Yen Tzu came to offices in which they could earn the popularity and the support of the people, and control the government of their states. Their fame and popularity spread beyond the narrow limits of their particular states, and they were in fact able to exert some influence on the international political scene. Shu Hsiang was the counsellor of Tsin, the confederacy leader: Yen Tzu was the prime minister of Ch'i, a state which had previously held the position of head of the alliance of the states of the central plain. However, Cheng, Tzu Ch'an's state, was small and weak, in no way comparable with Tsin and Ch'i, and it is very unexpected that the premier of such a state should come to possess so influential a voice in international political matters. Hsiang Hsü, the chief minister of Sung, had, a little before the time of the rise of Tzu Ch'an, wielded great influence in the field of diplomacy in Ch'un-ch'iu China, and Sung was, like Cheng, a small kingdom of the central plain. The international situation of the times, if carefully examined, reveals the reason why the chief officials of such small, and apparently insignificant states, could in this way make their influence felt in international diplomacy.

At this time, the city-states (the so-called twelve states of the Ch'un-ch'iu period), were ranged into two great power groups, in the north, the league of Tsin, and in the south, the league headed by Ch'u. Throughout the Ch'un-ch'iu period, there was a continued fierce struggle, and almost a pre-ordained opposition between the two confederacies. However, just before the period here under discussion, in 546 B.C., at the instigation of Hsiang Hsü, the famed minister of Sung, a state which had become the inevitable point of collision between the two power groups, the various states of China, wearied by the long years of savage inroads and fighting, were convened for an interstate peace conference, and an armistice agreement concerning interstate warfare was reached between the two leagues.

Unhappily, this agreement broke down in less than ten years and aggressive war began once again; yet, compared with conditions before the pact, the international situation was more settled: the danger of a full-scale war had receded a little, and a period of comparative peace was ushered in. The preservation of a state of equilibrium between the two leagues of Tsin and Ch'u formed the basis from which such conditions grew, and it was on the initiative of the smaller states such as Sung, Cheng, and Ch'en, whose territory lay on the plain and at the meeting point of the spheres of influence of the two powers, that this international situation was put to good use, and the two leader states skilfully manipulated. A compromise was reached, which led in turn to a period of comparative peace. The pathfinder in these moves was the premier of Sung, Hsiang Hsü, and it was Tzu Ch'an of Cheng who still more skilfully made use of this state of equilibrium between the two leagues

78

created by his predecessor, and who became the central figure of the international convention of the states of the plain. It was as a direct result of the temporary balance of power that Tzu Ch'an became the representative figure of the period of administration by wise and worthy ministers in the history of the central plain states.

Finding himself in this situation, Tzu Ch'an first aimed to utilize the peace in an attempt to generate an economic recovery in Cheng, for she had been completely debilitated by constant internal disorders, and by the alternating raids and inroads of the Tsin and Ch'u leagues. Cheng had been obliged to offer tribute to each of the leagues in return for her policy of reconciliation between them. Tzu Ch'an headed a mission to each of the leader states, and by his erudition and eloquence he succeeded in securing the lightening of this burden to an absolute minimum. However, an agreed and recognized minimum payment had to be made, and to this end, Tzu Ch'an first set in order land divisions and boundaries, levied additional property taxes, and encouraged economies in the expenditure of the people: with the surplus thus gained, he worked and planned for an increase in agricultural productivity. However, for the strong and firm promotion of his measures for economic recovery, it was essential to be able to enforce his policy by law. In enacting his laws, he had them inscribed on newly recast bronze vessels, such as those employed in festivals in honour of the ancestors. This was an important development, for it constituted the first form of codified law in China.

Previously, in the cities of the Ch'un-ch'iu kingdoms formed with the tribe as the basis, all administrative problems common to the different clans had been decided and resolved in convention by the leading

79

families of the more important clans. The execution of a decision thus made was guaranteed by a contract witnessed by the blood of the nobles of each party. Crimes involving only members of a single clan were under the jurisdiction of the particular clan involved, but any violation of the law which involved different clans became a matter for such a convention, the majority of the cases being settled by the payment of an indemnity. There existed only *ad hoc* settlements for solving a dispute involving two or more clans, and there was no determined written law, the principles of which underlay such settlements. Procedure of this nature, allowing a liberal share of autonomy to the clan, was idealized by later Confucian scholars under the guise of the term 'government by virtue', whereas Tzu Ch'an's innovation of enforced obedience to a written code was implicitly criticised by the appellation 'legalism'. Idealistic and theoretical verbal battles of this nature did not arise until much later, yet this formulation of a written code did cause a great stir among the noble classes of the kingdoms of the central plain. Tzu Ch'an is said to have received a communication of protest from Shu Hsiang, the eminent statesman of Tsin, defending the principle of clan autonomy within the system of the aristocratic government of the city-state.

However, to maintain Cheng's peaceful relations, especially with the leader states of the two leagues, it was essential to ensure a revenue to the state sufficient to pay her tribute. For this end, it was vital to increase agricultural productivity, to modify further the taxation system, and to introduce some machinery for the levying of taxes from the general body of the people, apart from those attached to the main clans. To ensure the penetration to the common people of his administrative measures, the only available means open to Tzu Ch'an lay in a break with the long-standing tradition of clan autonomy, and the institution of his codified law, which was then to be publicly proclaimed. In the beginning, Tzu Ch'an's revolutionary measures met with ill-will from his own people, and with strong criticisms from abroad, but, after three years had passed, and an increase in agricultural productivity had been realized, the earlier malignity turned to admiration and support.

To promote economic well-being, Tzu Ch'an had regulated agricultural holdings, and by his promulgation of a codified law, and the negation of the principle of the autonomy of the clan, he had set in motion a political and economic revolution. He thus appears as one who had already brought considerable criticism to bear on the traditional and time-honoured theory of the government of the city-state by an aristocracy of birth. A progressive in the political sphere, Tzu Ch'an's rational revolution was matched by his rationalist condemnation of tradition in the field of thought.

I have already explained that the city-states of ancient China were communities gathered together for the purpose of common religious celebration. In such communities, no distinction was made between the functions of church and state, between government and religion. Government was to be practised in accordance with the will of Heaven, and from this idea arose the problem of the means by which this will of Heaven could be known. Belief in a spirit or god, a personification and deification of Heaven, was for the most part shattered in the course of the Ch'un-ch'iu period, and in its place, there already existed in some measure the idea that Heaven was not a human being possessed of a form; Heaven's will was to be revealed in the will of humankind in general.

In other quarters, however, the belief still persisted that the will of the spirits should be discovered by magical arts and practices. In the time of the Yin dynasty, there was a flourishing practice of the magic art of tortoise shell divination, by which Heaven's will was determined through a study of the cracks appearing in a tortoise shell after the application of heat. Such divination by tortoise shell was inherited also by the Chou house, and even in Ch'un-ch'iu times, it remained as a part of the national tradition to the extent that, at the declaration of a vital war, the choice of the general was left to a decision formulated by close reference to the indications of tortoise shell divination. Apart from the labour of preserving and preparing the tortoise shells, there was the additional inconvenience caused by the burning processes: it is not surprising that, in actual fact, the employment of such divinatory methods in conjunction with state affairs was restricted to matters of very great moment to the community such as a decision to declare war.

Side by side with tortoise shell divination was the other magic art of divination by the milfoil practised in this period. In this further method, the deciding factor was the number of strips of yarrow leaf extracted from a bunch, which had been cut and fashioned in the form of thin strips the shape of a pencil. Originally, this was regarded as supplementary to the art of divination by tortoise shell, but it gradually developed into an independent art, entirely divorced from that of the tortoise shell, and in the Ch'un-ch'iu period, because of the less complicated nature of its processes, it became the more frequently employed method for discovering the import of the will of Heaven. This extraction of slips of plant from a bunch, and the decision of a point at issue by number, together with the adoption of quite complicated calculations based on the regular figures of the calendar, such as the number of months in a year, or of days in a month, and the forging of a connection between this art and the movements of the heavenly bodies, all combined to make divination by the milfoil a far more artificial mysticism than the simple prediction of Heaven's will by an inspection of the cracks appearing in a heated tortoise shell. The latter, also, was essentially a form of mysticism, but it was as yet unadulterated: in the case of the milfoil method, however, in consequence of its adaptation to the science of numbers, which was developing rapidly because of its intimate connection with the calendar, and the need for improved and more accurate methods of calculation in that sphere, there was a further advancement into a form of metaphysics based on number. Yet however far it developed, and despite its tendency to become a mathematical science, in so far as it was viewed as a means for the revelation of the will of Heaven, it remained a kind of sorcery.

In addition, celestial phenomena such as solar eclipses, weather indications of wind and rain, manifestations from the animal world such as the movements of birds in flight, or the damage caused by locusts, even manifestations man-made such as conflagrations, were all interpreted as indications of Heaven's will. Any unusual phenomenon of the natural and human worlds was viewed as a presage of harm about to be inflicted by Heaven on mankind.

In 524 B.C., a violent typhoon struck the central plain, and was followed by a destructive fire in four states, which included Sung and Cheng. The preceding year, the Master of Divination in Cheng had predicted this fire from astronomical indications, and had urged his prime minister Tzu Ch'an to attempt to avert any harm by immediate and continued sacrifice, but the latter had refused and ignored the advice. After the great fire, when the Divination Master predicted yet another conflagration, every citizen of Cheng, whether high or low, was affected by considerable panic, some even going as far as to suggest the transfer of the state capital to some less ill-omened site. But Tzu Ch'an merely countered with the words, 'Heaven's way is far removed: it is man's way that is near to us'—by which he meant that the way of man, the principle controlling the human world, is near, and can be understood by man; whereas Heaven's way, that is, the will of Heaven, is something far removed, and incomprehensible—a fact which a human diviner should have realized. However, since the Master of Divination was for ever making all manner of predictions, there were bound to be some occasions, as in the present instance, when his predictions would turn out correctly, although this was not to be taken as proof of invariable and unerring accuracy. To the end, Tzu Ch'an persistently refused to heed the advice, and it is recorded that, after all, there was no second conflagration in Cheng.

About two months after the great fire, Tzu Ch'an is said to have recited a lengthy litany in the course of a sacrificial ceremony to the spirit of the soil. He may well have believed in the efficacy of Heaven's will in bringing damage to the natural and human worlds. The opinion held by the Master of Divination and the people of Cheng in general was that while events of the human world could be foreknown to a certain extent, it was difficult to presage any event of disaster occurring by the will of Heaven. Tzu Ch'an however, made a clear distinction between the way of Heaven (that is, the supra-human world) and the way of man, and his attitude contained the seeds of rationalism, and a recognition that a distinction should be made by reason between what can be known and what is unknowable. The careful reader will not have failed to notice that at the base of his legalistic revolution in politics, there lay an undercurrent of a rationalist spirit. In the history of the thought of ancient China, Tzu Ch'an plays the important part of the first thinker in any way to escape from superstition, and move towards enlightenment; one of the peculiar characteristics of these years of government by wise and worthy ministers, is this sudden rise of rationalism and enlightenment.

This development spelt the end of the unity of religion and government in the joint sacrificial communities which formed the city-state, and the independence of the clans which had secured important positions within the state became less firm. The establishment of a code of written law implied a division of function, and a separation of the spheres of government and religion. Again, the distinction of the way of Heaven, as being an unknowable entity, from the way of man which was something that could be known, meant the separation of religion from learning. In fact, every new social tendency revealed in this age of worthy ministers can be understood as exemplifying this keynote of enlightenment. Although it was by no means fully developed, these years saw the birth of a consciousness of human nature.

3 Confucius' Attitude to his Predecessors

As I have argued above, the period of Confucius' life up to the age of thirty—that is, the formative years of study—coincided exactly with the time of the activity of Tzu Ch'an, the representative of the years of 'rule by a worthy minister'. There is a tradition, appearing in the biography of Confucius in the 'Historical Records', that in his youth, Confucius received a carriage and a team of horses from the prince of Lu, and journeyed far to the west to the capital of Chou (which lay on the site of the present-day Lo-yang), there to meet Lao Tzu, his elder in learning, and to question him about the ritual. If this story be true, Confucius would have had an opportunity of meeting with Tzu Ch'an, for the state of Cheng lay across the direct route of this journey to Lo-yang. However, Taoism developed later than Confucianism, and there is even doubt concerning the historicity of its reputed founder Lao Tzu. This story must be discountenanced as nothing more than one aspect of the attempt to link the personages of Confucius and Lao Tzu. Confucius' visit to the state of Ch'i at the age of thirty-six seems to have been his first trip abroad from Lu, and it thus appears that he was offered no opportunity of a face-to-face meeting with Tzu Ch'an (who, it will be remembered, died when Confucius was aged thirty-one).

Confucius visited Ch'i at the prime of his life, and although the duration of his stay is not clearly demarcated, he nevertheless remained some time there. During his stay, he is recorded as having an audience of the ruler of Ch'i, Duke Ching, with whom he discussed the morality of relations between a prince and his ministers. This conversation is recorded in a chapter of the so-called 'Later Analects'—the section of the work which was compiled at a later date—and there is thus considerable doubt whether this discussion is faithfully recorded.* Confucius was as yet the unknown son of an impoverished warrior knight, so that it seems probable that he was not at this juncture granted an interview

* Vid. inf. p. 103, for a full discussion of the text of the 'Analects.'

with Duke Ching. Further, it is likely that on this occasion, he did not meet with Yen Tzu, the first minister of Ch'i, although he does appear often to have heard talk of this popular statesman, for in the 'Analects' is recorded Confucius' statement, 'Yen P'ing-chung (i.e. Yen Tzu) knew well how to make a friend, and no matter how long the acquaintance lasted, he still showed the same degree of respect.' At a later juncture, when he had become an important official as Minister of Crime, Confucius accompanied his prince, Duke Ting, to a conference with Duke Ching of Ch'i. In the course of the conference, he saw through a ruse of Ch'i to stage a dance of eastern tribesmen, and to cow the Lu representatives by a show of military might, and severely reprimanded both Duke Ching and his premier Yen Tzu. (The story is told in all three commentaries of the 'Ch'un-ch'iu'). There is a degree of exaggeration in the narrative, but Yen Tzu although a forerunner of Confucius, does seem to have outlived Tzu Ch'an, and it is perhaps a fact that he did have the opportunity to meet Confucius, after the latter had become a Lu official.

There are quite a number of passages in the 'Analects' where Confucius comments on the famous statesmen of the Ch'un-ch'iu period. Among them, there are four references to the achievements of Kuan Chung, the minister of Duke Huan of Ch'i, who gathered the states of the central plain and established the northern league as a defence against the raids of the alien tribes. Next to him, in point of the number of references, comes Tzu Ch'an, who is spoken of three times. The benefactions of Kuan Chung through his measures in assistance of Duke Huan of Ch'i, are described by Confucius in the words, 'Had there been no Kuan Chung, we should now be wearing our hair unbound, and wearing our dress folding to the left; down to the present day, the people are still enjoying the benefactions he conferred.' By this was meant that, had not Kuan Chung put up a defence against the barbarians, the people of China would assuredly be wearing their hair and their dress in the manner of the barbarians. Then, there are the discussions about Tzu Ch'an; in a passage referring to Kuan Chung of Ch'i, Tzu Hsi, the premier of the state of Ch'u, and Tzu Ch'an, it is said, 'Someone asked about Tzu Ch'an, and the Master replied, "He was a kind man": to a question about Tzu Hsi, he replied, "Oh! That man!", and to one about Kuan Chung, he said, "He was the kind of man such that when he seized the city of P'ien, with its three hundred households, from the Po family, the head of the latter though forced to eat coarse food, and live a life of poverty, never uttered a single word of resentment."' Tzu Hsi is rejected as not worthy of treatment in this company, although Tzu Ch'an is regarded as worthy of being ranged alongside Kuan Chung. While the former is richly endowed with fellow-feeling, it is urged that even though Kuan Chung dealt with men strictly, such was his greatness that they would acquiesce in such treatment, and even unto death never make any complaint. In comparison with Kuan Chung, Tzu Ch'an is the lesser figure, although he is still of a stature such as to classify him with the former. It is evident that Confucius held Tzu Ch'an in great esteem, as his elder and senior.

Confucius, then, inherited the spirit of the period of the wise and worthy official, as it was exemplified in Tzu Ch'an, a person for whom he thus clearly felt some degree of reverence. We must now ask precisely what it was that Confucius inherited from the earlier period, and in what way he developed what he adopted. A closer examination of the differences of environment between Tzu Ch'an and Confucius is essential for the clarification of issues such as the definition of the latter's criticisms of the age of 'sage ministers', and the construction, in consequence of such criticisms, of his own position.

Tzu Ch'an came of a ducal family of the group of the 'Seven Mu' who traced their origin back to a prince of Cheng, Duke Mu. Although his particular family was comparatively weak within the 'Seven Mu', Tzu Ch'an was nevertheless the son of a noble, and born into a family sufficiently illustrious to qualify him for high office. In contrast, although Confucius' ancestors were said—perhaps with some amount of exaggeration—to have been descended from a ducal family of the state of Sung, they soon fled their native state, and after the move to Lu by the member four generations before Confucius, fell considerably in social standing. After the move to Lu, the K'ung family kept moving its residence within the country areas, and Confucius was in fact the son of a country knight, Shu-liang Ho, who had achieved some notoriety in his state on account of his military exploits. On the other hand, Tzu Ch'an was born into a family of high quality, his upbringing was that of a noble's son, with a long tradition behind it: what sort of an impression would this background make on Confucius, the son of an impoverished warrior, born into a poor and cold household, harried by the worries of eking out a mean living, and struggling throughout his youth to acquire knowledge?

Of Tzu Ch'an, Confucius said 'He had four of the virtues of the princely man: to himself, he was humble; in serving a superior, he was respectful; in fostering his people, he was kind, and in employing his people, he was upright.' Although born to the high status of a ducal family, he was yet modest and never arrogant or overweening; he was extremely zealous for the welfare of his people, and the betterment of their economic conditions, and he was moderate in employing them for military and forced labour duties in the service of the community. There was no taint in him of the arrogance which precludes the treatment of man as man, or of a contempt for superiors, or of the complete lack of fellow-feeling for those inferior to him—all of which were common faults and failings of the noble classes of his day. In fact, he was the ideal type of what the noble should be.

Confucius was able to refer to this Tzu Ch'an, the ideal noble, by the term of praise, 'princely man'. This term is used with varying significance in the 'Analects'. The first usage that should be noted is in contrast to the term 'mean man'—the country yokel, ignorant of the rules of ritual, and lacking any training in music: in contrast, the 'princely man' signifies the noble, residing in the city, where there was some knowledge of the ritual, and a taste for music. Again, the word is used to point the contrast with the 'mean man', occupied in tilling the fields, living in a rural community, who knew nothing of the wide world, and who, with no voice in politics or in administration, was of the number of the oppressed: in comparison, the 'princely man' was not himself concerned with the labours of agriculture, nor was his outlook confined to the narrow society of a village district, for the term rather indicates the noble living in the metropolis, and entering into all the activities of a broad political society. The 'princely man' is one completely equipped with the careful upbringing which befits a man of the status of a noble—he is the ideal of a cultured man of noble birth: thus Tzu Ch'an, the representative figure of the age of 'sage ministers', is the ideal of this cultured noble. Once Confucius imagined the processes of government in Cheng, with Tzu Ch'an at the centre; 'If an order were to be promulgated, P'i Ch'en would be entrusted with the compilation of the rough draft, after which an examination and discussion of its contents would be led by Shih Shu: Tzu-yü, a legate, would polish the style, and Tzu Ch'an of Tung-li would add a final embellishment'. That is, only after Tzu Ch'an, whose residence was in Tung-li, inside the walls of the capital of Cheng, had added his own final polishing of the style, would any edict be generally promulgated. Any decree born of the combined skill of such a number of wise ministers would be a well-considered measure, and would receive the warm welcome of the common people, with the result that it could be put into effect with no obstructions. Everything ran smoothly in the cabinet of Cheng, which was constituted by election from among the more talented members of the noble classes: it was sufficient for Tzu Ch'an, at its head, merely to take charge of the addition of rhetorical flourishes to the text of any proposed edict. Here, his talents appear more than anything to have been those of a stylist.

Fortunate in the two events, on the international field, the balance of power between the north and south leagues, and internally, the state of equilibrium between the powerful families of Cheng, the cabinet of Cheng, with Tzu Ch'an at its head, ushered in a period of efficient aristocratic government. But this balance of power was no more than a temporary state, and presently, various social and international factors began to emerge, and cause the breakdown of the beneficial structure built by the 'worthy ministers'.

First, in the sphere of international relations, after the failure of the peace settlement in mid-Ch'un-ch'iu times

91

between the two leagues, there still remained for a short time a situation in which the balance of power restrained the forces of the four great powers—the two leagues, and Ch'i in the east, and Ch'in in the west. In such an atmosphere, the wise ministers availed themselves of the comparatively peaceful conditions prevailing to further the development of the spirit of enlightenment. However, in the age of Confucius, a generation or so afterwards, the newly risen barbarian kingdoms of the south, first Wu, and then, in close succession, Yüeh, began to encroach on the central plain, and to grasp at the hegemony of China. The alarm had sounded once more for a crisis threatening Chinese civilization.

Throughout the early and middle years of the Ch'un-ch'iu period, the state of Ch'u had also constituted an ever-present menace to the kingdoms of the central plain. Ch'u was considered to be of southern barbarian stock, and did herself admit to such an origin. However, with this advance to the north, and contact with the various states of the plain, there came a gradual assimilation of the culture of the 'Han' people of the plain. In the words of the proverb, 'Ch'u's genius was put to good use by Tsin': that is, that there were not a few talented members of the state of Ch'u who were induced to leave their native land and accept posts as important officials in Tsin. In fact, by the time of the middle of the Ch'un-ch'iu period, there was no very great difference between the culture of Ch'u, and that of the central plain.

The case was quite different with the two powers of Wu and Yüeh, which, in the later years of the period, began to push their influence north up to the territory of the central states, though there was the tradition that the ancestor of the people of Wu was T'ai Po of Chou. However, the lineage of the ruling line apart, the very long period of residence in this territory south of the Yang-tzu would induce in the people an assimilation with the local mores, and they may perhaps be regarded as of an alien stock. The force of Ch'u's infiltration to the north was for the moment reduced by the rise of these new barbarian kingdoms, but as their own northward pressure in turn grew more and more insistent, the civilization of the kingdoms of the plain was once again faced with the threat of barbarian inroads. Lu especially, by virtue of its position astride the main route of communication, was open to the frontal attacks of both Wu and Yüeh, in their advance towards the plain. This menace from the southern barbarians, coupled with heavy pressure from her northern neighbour Ch'i, brought great hardships on Confucius' native state.

As for the internal conditions of the states of the plain, there had been a considerable change, especially in social and political matters, since the time of Tzu Ch'an. Throughout the Ch'un-ch'iu period, frequent disturbances had occurred in the various states over the problem of the succession to the throne, and these had often proved the spark to set alight internal disorders. Those noble families who regarded the position of premier or the other important offices as their hereditary prerogative, gradually came to possess all the actual authority vested hitherto in the feudatory princes, so that in fact, by the time of the middle years of the Ch'un-ch'iu period, the government of all the city-states had been completely appropriated by a few powerful family groups, and the ruler became no more than a puppet manipulated at the whim of these families. At this time, the city-states were controlled by an oligarchy of the nobles; the 'age of wise and worthy ministers' does in fact constitute the last few years of the life of this oligarchy. The balance of power between the various powerful noble families may well be explained as the outcome of the fact that they, blessed with political power and economic well-being, were yet unable to bring control of the administration entirely into their own hands, and compromised on handing over the reins of government to able heads of weaker families. The balance of power, again, may be viewed as a symptom of the beginning of the tottering of the foundations of the oligarchy of the powerful noble families.

During the course of the period of the 'sage ministers', there was a tendency for the actual control of the government, which had before this passed from the ruler to the powerful family head, further to pass to the hands of the retainers of such powerful families, who were usually members of the newly arisen class of military knights. This tendency became more prominent at about the time of Confucius, and by it, the influence of the powerful families became less effective. In Lu, the principal retainer, or steward, of the Chi family, the most powerful of the three influential families called the 'Three Huan', a man by the name of Yang Hu meddled in matters concerning the succession of the Chi family, and even held a position of such influence that he could attempt to grasp the reins of authority in Lu. In considering this Yang Hu as a typical representative of the newly developed class of military knights, it should be remembered that it was to this social group that Confucius belonged.

We should now ask what attitude Confucius, born into this class of military knights, adopted towards the legacy of the previous age of 'sage ministers', a generation before him. I have said above that he felt a genuine esteem for the great figure of the age, Tzu Ch'an: yet the son of the military knight must have felt some yearning—deriving from a feeling of inferiority about the difference in social status—for the position of the scion of the high-born noble family. Any feeling of reverence for Tzu Ch'an would naturally spring from a proper appraisal of his outstanding qualities as a man: yet at the base of Confucius' mind, there would be an unconscious undercurrent of feelings of deep longing for the upbringing and education, which seemed to come to the noble classes by mere right of birth.

Such motives apart, Confucius called Tzu Ch'an a princely man, and extolled his virtues. This term 'princely man', as I have explained above, connoted the ideal noble, or the ideal of a man with a noble's upbringing. Confucius for the time accepted this definition of the 'princely man', but was not prepared to abide by this acceptance without limit or condition.

FOUR

THE VIEWS OF CONFUCIUS

1 Man as a Social Being

Confucius adopted this term 'princely man', with its significance of the ideal noble personality, and prescribed it as the goal of the ideal personality to which one should strive to attain by self-cultivation. Whenever he talked of morality, he always discussed it in terms of the moral virtues with which the 'princely man' should be equipped. Confucius used the word 'princely man' on very many occasions in the 'Analects'—in fact it appears more than seventy times,—but as the 'Analects' is a record of the dialogues which took place between Confucius and his disciples, rather than a systematized book, there is never given a clear-cut definition of the term, which is used with different nuances, which vary with the context and the person of the party to the conversation.

A rough division of these differing nuances reveals that the first function of the term is to distinguish the 'princely man' from the country yokel, that is, from the common people; here, the term indicates the ideal of the nobleman. Again, in the statement, 'The princely man possesses no manual abilities', the intended meaning is that the 'princely man' is not one who is a master of any technical skills, but one who has received a wide-reaching gentleman's education. It was this latter kind of education which the group centred on Confucius aimed to provide. In this concept of the 'princely man' and the goal of a completely novel education, there was a contrast between the class of knights, who, by virtue of some specialized technique, served in government posts, or took service with noble families, and earned their living by means of such a calling, and the noble classes who did not need to worry over their livelihood because of the estates inherited from their forebears, and could devote their entire attention to administration and the related matter of religious observances. And for this reason, there still remained on the part of the nobles an attitude which amounted to contempt for any man forced to follow a vocation. All such ideas and considerations were included, whether directly or indirectly, in the concept of the ideal noble of the age of 'sage ministers', though examples of the use of the term 'princely man' with this connotation are comparatively rare in the 'Analects'.

In the second place, there is the idea of the 'princely man' as described in the words, 'The princely man does not seek to fill his belly, or to rest in contentment. He is diligent in his actions, his words are prudent: he deals on the square with those who are possessed of the Way, and he is one who loves learning.' He is then one who gives no mind to the luxury of his daily life, who has put academic discussions behind him, and seeks to put his words into practice; who questions his virtuous elders about any doubts, and who has a zest for study. This use of the term as the mark of a practical education does in fact account for the majority of its occurrences in the 'Analects'. If the earlier usage indicates the ideal human being brought up to be a gentleman, this later use signifies the disciple undergoing a moral education. Yet this concept of the scholar prepared to devote his life to such moral upbringing is never met with before the time of Confucius. It was he who transformed the idea of the 'princely man' as the ideal of the education in good taste of noble society into the concept of the scholar sacrificing his life to the pursuit of a moral training.

The earlier usage indicated a complete man, who had already acquired his education, but this later connotation points to an incomplete personality, possessed of some sort of goal, and in search of education. The point we should now discuss concerns the nature of the studies the 'princely man', in this latter sense, would pursue in the attainment of his object.

In Confucius' words, ' The "princely man" makes a wide study of the literature, and has the ritual with which to bind such studies.' The word 'literature' here, as I have already explained, points to the 'Odes' and the 'Documents', topics of study which the education of a knight of the time could not afford to neglect. The culture of the old Chou house, or at least, what remained of that culture, was contained in these two books (although of course, by the word 'book' is not necessarily meant only material written down in book form, for there would be included with this an amount of material taught by oral tradition). However, it would not be satisfactory simply to read books of the style of the 'Odes' and the 'Documents' and merely to absorb knowledge thus. Such book knowledge must be something which accompanied actual practice. In saying that such knowledge should be bound into a whole by the ritual, Confucius meant that the practising of the conventions of the ritual would render such knowledge a much more assuredly personal possession. The earlier quotation of Confucius' precept, 'be diligent in action, and circumspect in your words', with its emphasis on actual practice, is quite the same in meaning.

Now what was the aim of the 'princely man'—the goal he sought to achieve by this study of the literature and practice of the ritual? Confucius says, 'If a man have in him no "humanity", what can he have to do with ritual, or with music?' That is, if a man study the ritual and music, if he does not have this quality of 'humanity', it is all to no purpose. This being so, 'humanity' is something much more basic and fundamental than even the ritual, and both ritual and music are, in fact, a kind of manifestation of this paramount 'humanity', and are one means by which it is to be realized. 'Humanity' is the supreme virtue, and the most fundamental principle advocated by Confucius. Of the 'princely man', Confucius said that he would not seek after wealth and honour, would not be oppressed by poverty and a mean station, for he does not desert 'humanity' even for the space of a single meal: in moments of haste, in times of danger, he remains steadfast in 'humanity';—for, 'if the "princely man" desert "humanity", he will on no account fulfil the demands of his station.'

The aim of the 'princely man' in his life on earth, is closely bound up with the attainment of 'humanity'. Confucius also says, 'There are some, to be classed as "princely men" who have not attained to "humanity", but I have never heard of a "mean man" who has achieved it', by which he seems to have indicated that the scope of the term 'princely man' is not necessarily limited to one who has already attained to 'humanity'. However, these words are contained in the 'Later Analects', which came into being at a somewhat later period. The 'princely man' studies literature, practises ritual, and never for an instant departs from 'humanity'. He is always striving to attain to the realization of 'humanity', and the term does not include the one who has already achieved it to perfection and in entirety.

What then was this highest good, this 'humanity' to

Confucius? The meaning of 'humanity' was the subject of constant questions to Confucius by the disciples, who were for ever enquiring the means of successfully realizing it, and were never able clearly to understand the replies. Naturally, the solution to the problem of the real meaning of 'humanity' cannot be regarded as at all easy for us, 2,500 years after the lifetime of Confucius, when even his contemporaries, the disciples who questioned him to his face, could not fully comprehend the import of his answers. For Confucius' disciples, both the theoretical problem of understanding the intrinsic nature of 'humanity', and the practical moral problem of the means of realizing it, were invariably regarded as inseparably interrelated. But though we might recognize the propriety of a view of theory and practice as a unity, by disregarding, for the moment, the aspect of practical morality, and by enquiring into the etymology of the term 'humanity', it might be possible to gain at least some insight into the solution of the problem.

There are frequent examples in Chinese literature of a confusion between the similar characters for 'humanity', and 'man'. For example, in the words, 'When one looks at the past, there one can know humanity', and, 'the zealous knight, and the benevolent man do no harm to humanity'—there are some texts where the character for 'humanity' has been replaced by that for 'man': the two were phonetically akin, and were used interchangeably in early times. This phonetic proximity indicates an original link in meaning of the two terms. Jen, 人, means man, men, or other men, and there are contexts where 'humanity', jen, 仁, signifies the feeling of affection entertained for others. Asked for a definition of 'humanity' by a disciple of the name of Fan Ch'ih, Confucius replied, 'It is to love others'.

To a question from Tzu Kung, one of the most talented disciples, on the problem why one should entertain feelings of goodwill toward others, phrased in the words, 'How about treating the people with extensive benefits, and helping the multitudes—can this be called "humanity"?' (these acts being such that even the sage rulers of olden times were unable to achieve them), Confucius replied, 'The man of "humanity", desiring to be established himself, seeks also to establish others: and the goals he wishes to attain himself, he helps others to gain. The way of "humanity" is to be able to see others by a rule near to oneself.' In other words, the man who has attained 'humanity', in any assertion of his own claims, acts only after recognizing the claims of others.

Tzu Kung once asked if there was a single word to act as a guide to conduct for a lifetime. In reply, Confucius suggested the word 'reciprocity', which he defined as, 'What you do not wish to be done to you, do not do to others.' Reciprocity is the ability to project one's feelings into others, and to put oneself into the other's position. Again, another disciple, Tseng Tzu, regarded the Way of Confucius as definable in terms of 'loyalty and reciprocity only.' That is, his Way was revealed in the general precepts of loyalty and reciprocity. Chu Hsi, the famous Sung scholar, explained this passage by the words, 'Exhausting oneself is what is called loyalty, projecting oneself into others is what is meant by reciprocity.' What Confucius meant by loyalty was a fidelity to the self, complete absence of self-deceit, and a realization of one's own personality. The extension of this sense of loyalty to include the persons of others and the faculty of projecting one's own feelings into a second person is what he meant by reciprocity.

The 'reciprocity' offered by Confucius to Tzu Kung as the virtue which should govern one's entire conduct, and Tseng Tzu's definition of the Way of Confucius in terms of loyalty and reciprocity, are in fact both a means of understanding what Confucius understood by the term 'humanity'. 'Humanity', synonymous with 'reciprocity', recognizes others as being human beings identical with the self, and implies the treatment of others as well as the self as being such. 'Humanity' is a self-realization of human beings, or loyalty; but since at the same time, the self is recognized not as an isolated individual but as existing in society along with other human beings, this loyalty should be transformed into the much broader and wider 'reciprocity': it is the self-realization not of the human being in isolation, but of the human being as a member of society. This term 'humanity' indicated the self-realization of man, or, in its most sublime sense, the self-realization of man in society. The attainment of 'humanity' was, for Confucius, the mission of the 'princely man': in his moral theory 'humanity' was regarded as the foundation of the other virtues, all of which were to be derived from this supreme first principle.

However, one matter to which attention should be drawn is that although Confucius to a certain extent consciously viewed 'humanity' as the self-realization of man in society, it cannot be said that he regarded it simply as a quality which could be broken down into the two simple elements of loyalty and reciprocity. On one occasion, Tzu Kung made the statement, 'What we do not wish to be done to us, we in our turn should not be willing to do to others'—a statement which is, in all aspects, identical with the definition of reciprocity given in Confucius' reply to a query by this same Tzu Kung on the matter of some virtue which might be a guide for a lifetime of action. Yet in spite of this, when he heard these words of Tzu Kung, of exactly the same import as his own definition of reciprocity, Confucius said, by way of a rebuke, 'You know, Tz'u' (Tzu Kung's given name) 'that is something which not even you can achieve.' Thus a maxim concerning reciprocity offered by Confucius to Tzu Kung in one chapter of the 'Analects', when repeated by the latter in another context, is condemned out of hand by Confucius, as an ideal too lofty for the other's attainment. This is the kind of anomaly in the 'Analects' which it is very difficult for the reader to comprehend.

In fact, the twenty chapters of the 'Analects' do not comprise Confucius' own writings on the subject of his own theories; they are the result of the compilation in book form by the disciples of their conversations with Confucius—with the disciples, in the great majority of cases, invoking their powers of memory for the task. Compilation of this nature was effected many times through the period lasting from the lifetime of Confucius' direct disciples to that of their disciples, or even later. The present text of the 'Analects' is a collection of different strata, compiled at differing periods and by men of diverging schools. The first ten chapters (called the 'Earlier Analects'), are considered to be comparatively early in date, while the latter ten chapters are thought to have been a fairly late compilation. According to the view of Doctor Takeuchi,* in a very detailed textual study of the 'Analects', except for chapters one, nine, and ten, the remaining seven chapters of the 'Earlier Analects' contain the oldest material. Chapter VI (in which Confucius condemns Tzu Kung's definition of reciprocity) is part of the material

*Note. Vid. Takeuchi Yoshio, Rongo no kenkyū (Study of the 'Analects'). Iwanami, Tokyo, 1939.

considered to be the oldest, and Chapter XV (where Confucius defines reciprocity and offers it as a rule of life), which is part of the 'Later Analects' is of a stratum compiled at a much later date.

If we incorporate the findings of this textual study, Confucius' rebuke in Chapter VI is a much more faithful representation of his views than the definition of reciprocity, and its function, offered by him in Chapter XV. Confucius thought, then, that the virtue of reciprocity, and the ability to project one's own mind into that of another, was not so very easily capable of realization by men; the rebuke of Tzu Kung does, in fact, come very near to the true feelings of Confucius on this point. The suggestion of reciprocity as a maxim by Confucius to Tzu Kung (in Chapter XV) might well be interpreted as a variation of the earlier conversation (in which Confucius administered the rebuke) which had crept in during the interval of the transmission of this conversation from Tzu Kung to his disciples (in fact two generations after Confucius)—a variation which persisted and grew to the extent that, in the end, the conversation was mistakenly understood as constituting the suggestion of the virtue of reciprocity to Tzu Kung by Confucius—in reality, the very opposite of the true circumstances.

Confucius himself regarded the virtue of reciprocity as not very easy of attainment. Thus the tradition in Chapter XV of the 'Analects', of Confucius himself expounding the virtue to Tzu Kung, should be considered to be an addition of the period when, as an explanation of 'humanity', the definition in terms of a separation into loyalty and reciprocity—which was the view of disciples such as Tzu Kung and Tseng Tzu —had gained vogue. The definition of 'humanity' as loyalty plus reciprocity could not be clearly or definitely established from the words of Confucius himself: hence its origin through the agency of disciples such as Tzu Kung.

Confucius considered that the 'princely man' whose mind is set on the attainment of 'humanity' should be freed from the narrow and inhibiting environment of his local village society, and be allowed independently to progress towards its realization. He said of the practice of 'humanity' that, 'When at ease in your home, you should be circumspect: in office, you should be respectful: in association with others, be loyal and sincere, and even though you be with the barbarians, you will not be abandoned'. The practice of 'humanity', then, should not be regarded as something remote, for the benefit of humankind in general; it should spring from prudence and circumspection in both word and act, in dealings with one's immediate family, one's relatives, and one's village friends—people, that is, with whom one is in daily contact.

For Confucius, this self-awakening of man in society begins with man regarded as a unit in a narrow family circle, widens to the concept of man as a unit among his relations, then as a unit in his village, and finally passes all bonds of distinction between races to become the self-awakening of man as a member of a world society. However, though this self-awakening of man as a member of society in general was an ultimate goal, and though it may have existed as a lofty ideal, it was yet felt to be something as yet unrealized and not in full being as far as concerned the matter of the day-to-day practice of morality. This being the case, the conception of 'humanity' as man's social awakening is never distinctly formulated in so many words by Confucius. The disciples, too, vaguely realized something of this significance of 'humanity'; but after some of them had sounded their master about his views on this matter, and had failed to secure any clearly stated and positive reply, the perennial problem of the definition of 'humanity', and their failure to reach any clear-cut solution of it, caused them many moments of anxious concern.

In Confucius' estimation, Tzu Ch'an possessed a deep fund of charity. As a statesman, he was full of consideration for the common people of Cheng, and beneath this concern, there must have been some latent store of 'humanity'—understood as the self-awakening of man in society. Tzu Ch'an was the kind to have assented to a free discussion of his policies in the local district school, and, a magnanimous statesman, he recognized the right of freedom of speech in politics. However, he would not countenance the interference of the general populace in one sphere only—in decisions affecting important matters of foreign policy, for he argued that the general plebs, that is the ' "mean man" is carried away by his hot-headedness to policies which court disaster; in instinctively seeking to make a name for himself, he loses sight of the interests of the state as a whole.' Thus, while Tzu Ch'an showed considerable affection for the masses of Cheng, he still considered that only the 'princely man'—the noble—was fit to pronounce on affairs of state; where the matter of reason was concerned, he failed to shake off the prejudice of the nobleman, that he, as opposed to the common man, was possessed of some innate superiority.

On this point, Confucius argued that, 'The "princely man" is knowledgable in matters where right is concerned, the "mean man" where profit is at issue.' The distinction between princely and mean is made to hang on the possession or lack of moral sense—or, again, this self-awakening of man in society. The difference lay in this moral sense, and not in any reasoning power, the presence or absence of which was conditioned by the status of one's birth. By his statement that, 'Only the very wise and the very stupid cannot be changed', Confucius seems to have recognized the fact of innate differences of mental capacity; yet he also argues that, 'I have yet to meet a man whose powers were insufficient to the task of applying himself for a whole day to "humanity" '—by which he indicated that, provided he have the necessary will, anyone may attain 'humanity'. The thought is further clarified by the words, 'By nature men are akin: it is practice that creates gaps between them': the moral sense is then an inherent quality, in which there are only minor differences, and it is through acquired training that there develops a distinction of any degree.

Tzu Ch'an saw the distinction between 'princely man' and 'mean man' as that of innate reasoning power, which the noble possessed, and the masses lacked: against this view, Confucius held that the distinction was one of moral sense—a difference which arose with acquired training. This divergence of viewpoint can well be understood as arising from the different attitudes of the man born as a member of the noble classes, and the son of the newly formed military knight class. Confucius said, 'The "princely man" cleaves to virtue, the "mean man" cleaves to the soil'—meaning that while the mass of the people cling for their entire lifetime to the old rural society into which they were born, the 'princely man' must part from this narrow and confining village society, and, in the environment of a broad and enlightened political society, live a life of unfettered activity. The following further statement has the same meaning, 'If a knight clings to an idle and retired life, he is not a fit person to bear the name of "knight" ', the only difference being the change of terminology from 'princely man' to 'knight'. Again,

'The zealous knight, and the man of "humanity" will not seek to live at the expense of doing harm to "humanity": rather would they kill themselves, to preserve their "humanity" complete'. This parallelism between the 'zealous knight' and the 'man of humanity' seems to indicate that it is 'humanity' on which the zealous knight's aim is set. In this sense, there is no distinction between the knight and the 'princely man' whose target is 'humanity'—although it should be noted that the contexts in the 'Analects' where 'knight' is used as synonymous with 'princely man' are invariably in the chapters of the 'Later Analects'.

Tseng Tzu, one of the group of younger disciples (which included men like Tzu Chang, Tzu Yu, Tzu Hsia) once said, 'A man who could be entrusted with an orphan prince, who could be given a fief of a hundred li, who is not to be snatched away from his lofty principles —is such a one a "princely man"? Yes, indeed he is'. Immediately following is the statement, ' The knight should be strong and firm, for his burden is heavy and his way long. "Humanity" is his burden; is it not heavy? Only with death does his course stop; is not that long?' The knight then regards the attainment of 'humanity' as his lot, and even unto death must he unflinchingly carry through with his task. This term 'knight' used by Tseng Tzu is in no respect different from the 'princely man' of the previous statement: both must, even at the cost of death, persevere in the attempt to attain to 'humanity'. For the particular school of Confucianism headed by Tseng Tzu, the terms 'knight' and 'princely man' are completely identical.

In this way, the earlier concept of the 'princely man' as the model human being with the elegant upbringing of the noble has for Tseng Tzu been changed to the model of the class of knights, in the service of a prince or a noble family, and possessed of talents called on by the ruler. It may well be that the use of the terms 'knight' and 'princely man' as synonyms is the result of a later exegesis, and corrections and additions from the hand of either Tseng Tzu or of the pupils of the time—the disciples of the original disciples. The transition to the point of regarding the 'princely man' as the ideal pattern of the class of knights, cultivating military rather than civil virtues, is symptomatic not of the age in which Confucius lived, but of the lifetime of his disciples. Hence it should be surmised that the transition from regarding the 'princely man' as the model pattern of the class of nobles, to that of the knight, was fully effected in the time of the disciples, although it may well be that a trend in this direction was at least becoming evident even in Confucius' lifetime.

The first evidence of the concept of 'humanity', the self-awakening of man in society—is to be seen in the age of 'worthy ministers', but at this stage, the process and its effects were confined to the narrow limits of the noble classes. Confucius was the first to broaden the concept, and to extend its scope to include the newly arisen and more extensive class of knights, and it was by him that the concept of 'humanity' was really created. By the time of the disciples, the process of the self-awakening of the class of knights had become more precise, and the final outcome was the definition of 'humanity' in terms of the concepts of loyalty and reciprocity.

2 *The Divorce of Education from Religion.*

The age of 'sage ministers' of which Tzu Ch'an was the representative figure was the period of the first awakening of rationalism in the history of Chinese thought. Now in what way did Confucius treat the legacy of enlightenment from the age before him?

We ought first to examine Confucius' attitude to religion. Asked about knowledge by one of his disciples, Fan Ch'ih, he said, 'Strive for the execution of your duties to the people: respect the spirits, but keep them at a distance: this can be called knowledge.' Now in the early city-state communities, at the time when there still existed the unity of religion and administration, no division was made between the functions of governing the people, and the offering of religious celebrations in honour of the spirits. It was the administrative aspect of this dualism on which Confucius laid emphasis, and although at any religious celebration to a deity, he advocated polite sacrifice, and due respect for the object of the sacrifice, he rejected the combination of religion and government which had persisted since the time of the Yin kingdom, and by which any move affecting the state was effected only after ascertaining the will of the spirits. Confucius clearly and consciously felt the need for a divorce of religion from matters connected with government, and since he defined knowledge in terms of the recognition of this need, knowledge itself must also be separated and kept distinct from religion. Asked by Tzu Lu about the observance of service to the spirits, Confucius replied 'You cannot yet adequately serve men: how would you serve the spirits well?' At this, Tzu Lu went on further to question his master concerning death, to which Confucius replied, 'As yet you do not know what there is to know about life: why should you want to know about death?'

Tzu Lu was well known among the disciples for his daring and courage, for he was apt to be carried away by his spirit of adventure. Yet there was none who came near to him as far as concerned the intensity of his mental application in his search for truth. Any precept taught to him by Confucius, he would immediately and to the letter attempt to translate into action: thus it was said of him, 'When Tzu Lu heard some maxim, his only fear was that he would hear a second before he could put the first into deeds'.

However, an eager disciple of this nature would inevitably leave behind him many neglected and forgotten gaps in his wholehearted frontal assault on the truth. One day, Confucius called him by his given name and said to him, 'Yu, shall I teach you what knowledge is? It is a state wherein you are firm in the knowledge of what you do know, and admit to a lack of knowledge of what you do not know.' These words were by way of a warning to Tzu Lu against allowing his romantic impulses to rush him along to the adoption of some empty theory.

Confucius further said, 'An examination of the past brings an understanding of "humanity" ', and, 'If Hui', (the given name of Yen Yüan, one of the disciples) 'hears one point, from that he gains a knowledge of ten. If Tz'u', (the given name of Tzu Kung) 'hears one point, he knows two.' Knowledge then is gained by observation, and listening, and its roots spring from experience. However, the simple experience of observation does not of itself constitute knowledge: rather, 'listening widely, and selecting what is good from what one has heard, and following it, seeing much, and marking it down, this constitutes a kind of second-grade knowledge.' The type of knowledge then which comes from experience, and from a selection of what is good from among one's experiences, is not of the highest quality, but is nevertheless something akin to knowledge. Confucius modestly suggests that knowledge consists in the motion of selecting from one's visual and aural experience, and in the final analysis, knowledge consists in the ability to discriminate, evinced in this selection and promotion of what is found to be good from one's experience.

However, knowledge does not stop at a simple discrimination of the known from the unknown; if that were so, only matters already known would be given attention, and there would be no place for a widening of knowledge. Asked by Tzu Chang if the shape of the government of China ten generations hence could be known, Confucius replied, 'Yes: the Yin dynasty, in the formulation of its system of ritual, borrowed from that of the preceding Hsia dynasty, and one can work out what additions were made, and where any part was rejected. Similarly, Chou borrowed from the ritual system of Yin, and again, it is possible to discover what was added, and what rejected. Hence, whatever the date, be it even a hundred generations hence, one can know by inference the corpus of ritual of the royal line which succeeds to Chou.' Confucius believed that from the tendencies evinced in the changes introduced by the two dynasties of Yin and Chou into the previously existing systems of state ritual, could be inferred a general trend, and that this process of inference could be applied to a situation a hundred generations hence. For Confucius then, a good knowledge of history up to the present should be made the basis from which predictions concerning the trend of future events could be offered. Knowledge then is not simply a matter of what is already known, or the knowable: the known should be made a basis for an investigation into the unknown, the knowable for the unknowable. Only in the case of Tzu Lu did Confucius attempt to discourage the plan for an all-out investigation into the unknowable without making any distinction between the knowable and the unknowable.

Another point to which attention should be drawn is that while this conversation with Tzu Lu is recorded in a chapter which forms part of the 'Later Analects', the discussion with Fan Ch'ih quoted above (concerning the second-grade knowledge which comes from experience) is part of the 'Earlier Analects'. The former, albeit motivated by the desire to warn and restrain the impetuous Tzu Lu, yet contains a strong admixture of anti-religious feeling, in its condemnation of the worship of the spirits, while the latter, with its statement, 'show respect for the spirits, while still keeping them at a distance', preserves religion within its proper limits as religion, and exhibits the healthy and sound attitude of prohibiting its infringement into the sphere of government. Both statements, in fact, set limits on religion, but the former especially attracts attention by virtue of the fact that its attack on religion has become absolutist.

In the latter statement, the rationalist criticism of religion first enunciated by Tzu Ch'an is further clarified, and becomes, in Confucius' thinking, a rationalist attack on religion. In the 'Earlier Analects', apart from the discussion with Fan Ch'ih under review here, there is a further statement to Tzu Kung, who wished to do away with the ritual of reporting at the ancestral temple on the occasion of the first day of the month, a ritual accompanied by the sacrifice of a sheep. Confucius replied to the suggestion, 'Tz'u' (the given name of Tzu Kung), 'You may love the sheep, but I love the ritual.' Confucius, that is, had no feeling for the sacrificed animal, but only for the ritual of the sacrificial celebration, which he wished to preserve. The same chapter also contains a section in which it is recorded that whenever he entered the Great Temple, Confucius asked the officials there all manner of questions about procedure.

Thus, Confucius' attack on religion in the 'Earlier Analects' is not an all-out one: he is revealed as desiring, as far as was practical, the preservation of the ritual of public religious ceremonies in the city-state, in its original formal and correct form. However, in his time, alongside of this traditional and formal religious ritual, there had begun to flourish a widely practised new religion. Of this, Confucius said, 'To sacrifice to the spirits of ancestors not of one's own kin, is flattery. To see the right, and fail to do it, reveals a lack of valour.' This is severe criticism of the newly arisen religion, which called for sacrifice to the heterodox spirits discussed by the new sorcerers-in-chief—although sacrifice to the state deities, and celebrations in honour of the ancestor-spirits of the several noble families were exempted from this condemnation. And he dismissed as cowards, with no regard for the right, the fellow-travellers who subscribed to these new beliefs.

Confucius, again in the 'Earlier Analects', is said to have 'sacrificed to the dead as if they were present, and to the spirits as if they were present.' It is not that Confucius believed that the souls or the spirits of the deceased ancestors were possessed of some spiritual and superhuman powers, by which they could take control in any positive way over the events of the human world, nor is there any hint or suggestion that faith should be placed in, and use made of any such spiritual efficacy. Rather, the spirit is regarded as possessing a power equivalent to that of the man, and thus should be offered sacrifice with the same attitude of respect and deference as one would pay to any living man with whom one came in contact. Confucius tried to remove from the religious celebrations of the old city-state the legacy of mysticism, and of government by oracular predictions, and to introduce, in its stead, a body of religious ritual in which the concept of man took the central place.

Once, when Confucius was dangerously ill, Tzu Kung begged to be allowed to intercede for him, but Confucius stayed him with the words, 'My prayers have been offered over a long period.' It would serve no useful purpose, when Confucius was afflicted with a serious illness, to summon a prayer master, and to pray for recovery to some uncomprehending spirit, since Confucius had at all times offered prayers to those spirits to which sacrifice was made at regular state religious gatherings. To the disciples it appeared that, in normal times, and in his usual health, Confucius had never offered prayers to any spirit, but in fact, he had prayed to the regular spirits at state religious functions. Confucius did not reject religion out of hand; he was imbued with a deep religious faith in the traditional spirits recognized as orthodox by the state, and by the community in general.

By and large, Confucius took over the rationalist attitude to religion of which there were indications in the earlier age of Tzu Ch'an; he tried to establish this on the basis of an intrinsic religious appreciation, and attempted to preserve, in purified form, the religious festivals both for the traditional state deities, and for the family spirits. In Confucius' thinking, there was as yet not a complete escape from the influence of the religion of the nobles of the old-time city-states.

The placing of the distinction between the knowable and the unknowable in a cognition by reason, and the attitude that religious mysticism should be completely rejected as a part of the unknowable was finally given clear expression at the time of the compilation of the 'Later Analects', during the lifetime of Confucius' disciples, or their pupils. The complete divorce of learning from religion did not take place until after the time of Confucius, when any religious sentiments still alive in Confucius himself, had perished in the thinking of his disciples or scholars following him. Thus grew the doctrine of Confucianism, free from any religious admixture.

Confucius' theory that reason distinguishes between the knowable and the unknowable, should be viewed in connection with his compromise with the state and national religious celebrations, which were in themselves a form of mysticism. Knowledge, what he meant by reason, is invariably discussed in company with 'humanity', the practical reason by which a moral judgment is made. Thus, for example, Confucius says, 'The man of knowledge finds his pleasure in water, and the man of "humanity" in the hills: the man of knowledge is active, he of "humanity" is tranquil: the former is joyful, the latter long-lived.' This statement of the man of knowledge's fondness for water and the man of 'humanity's' fondness for the hills is symbolic of the former's activeness, and the latter's quietude, the man of 'humanity' being regarded as the more stable. From the words, 'the man of "humanity" rests in "humanity"', while the man of knowledge puts "humanity" to use', it appears that it is the man of 'humanity' who has really comprehended 'humanity', rather than the man of knowledge. The former is superior in that he is in a settled state. Simply to regard knowledge as knowledge, and to 'know that', is not adequate. It is by a direct application of knowledge to action that it becomes a virtue, or that it leads to 'humanity'. Knowledge is then a stepping stone leading to 'humanity' and Confucius clearly put practical reasoning, (i.e. his 'humanity') on a higher plan than pure reason, (his knowledge).

A verse of the 'Analects' mentions Confucius' attitude

to the traditional music: 'Confucius said of the Shao that it was the perfection of beauty and goodness: of the Wu he said that though perfect in beauty, it did not reach a point of ideal goodness.' The music of the ancient sage-ruler Shun, and that of the founder of the Chou house, King Wu, are here evaluated in terms of their beauty and goodness. Confucius made no rigorous distinction between beauty and goodness, and again, drew no clear line between the true and the good. He said, 'To know the truth is not as good as to love it, to love it is not as good as to delight in it.' Now knowledge is a matter for reason, loving and delighting in are both matters of taste, but Confucius treated them as being of the same class, and argued for a distinction of degree between them.

I have said above that one of the special features of the age typified by Tzu Ch'an was its tone of enlightenment. Enlightenment lays a stress on reason, and the period of Tzu Ch'an was one which saw the awakening of rationalism. Confucius inherited this outlook, and pushed the claims of reason, or knowledge, although for him, reason included both judgments of truth, and judgments of taste, and the latter were regarded as being of a higher value. This was because learning, and study, were regarded as the live and active mental processes of a man in action, and so the man of knowledge, as well as the man of 'humanity' were, in the final analysis, treated as persons engaged in some activity, that of living a highly worth-while creative life. In Confucius' eyes, it was Yen Hui who, among the disciples, evinced the greatest fondness for learning: he said of him, 'With a single dish of rice to eat, and a gourd dish of drink, living in a filthy hovel, while under such circumstances others could not have endured the distress, Hui did not allow his pleasure in life to be affected.' Yen

Hui, even in the circumstances of a poverty-stricken environment, found self-sufficiency in his love of learning. The search for knowledge and for 'humanity' was in fact identical with the search for the happy life. But the highest pleasures could not be found in either knowledge or learning, and only when the state of 'humanity' was reached was there a simultaneous attainment, in its fullest sense, of the happy life.

Confucius' rationalism was built on the foundation of this theory of pleasure, and so the originality of the role he gave to reason was not firmly established. Hence, the independence of learning from religion was of necessity incomplete. The fetters of the state religion were as yet not completely loosened, and in pursuance of this compromise, Confucius moulded such religious ceremonies as he desired to retain, to a newly moralized ritual. To Yen Yüan's question about 'humanity', Confucius replied, 'Humanity is to conquer oneself, and to return to the ritual.' 'Humanity' thus consists in the overcoming of one's desires, and in the following of the regulations of ritual. Ritual is something outside of the self, and so can serve to restrain the self, while 'humanity' is the acceptance of a law beyond oneself. This quotation is from a chapter in the 'Later Analects', and it may well be that the words do not reflect the true ideas of Confucius. He did, at any rate, think that the man who had been awakened to the fact of his social environment, and obligations, stood the best chance of constructing the happiest livelihood—and it was to the ordering of such a livelihood that he gave the term 'ritual'.

Confucius' rationalism paid due regard to ritual, and, more particularly during the lifetime of his disciples, there gradually emerged the tendency to compromise with tradition, and adapt ways of thinking so as to combine with it. In this sense, then, it would be fair to conclude that Confucius inherited the enlightenment of the age of Tzu Ch'an, but was unable to effect a thorough-going and perfected rationalism.

3 Criticism of Tradition

Although not entirely successful, Confucius did at least establish the claims of reason, by freeing learning from the mysticism of religion. Let us once again examine his statements concerning learning, and see what was the place of tradition in his theory of knowledge. One immediately thinks of the words, 'I transmit, and do not create: I believe in the past, and love it'; then again, 'I am not one of your people who claims innate knowledge. Rather, I love the past, and eagerly seek it out.' Confucius then did not set himself up as an individual and original scholar; he merely transmitted and expounded the doctrines of his forerunners. Thus, prima facie, it seems that his learning was a complete and blind subservience to the authority of tradition, and these words may well be understood as signifying his inability to escape in any way from the bonds of tradition. But these are statements by Confucius himself, a man always too modest concerning his own affairs and abilities, and we should be on our guard against accepting them at face value. The continuation of the first quotation above reads, 'To learn quietly, to study without being sated, and to teach others without flagging—such activities cause me no trouble.' Confucius thus argues, with firm self-confidence, that he can get on quietly with the task of learning and committing to memory the 'Odes', the 'Documents', and the Ritual, handed down from olden times, can learn from his tutor without satiety, and teach others without being wearied—and that such tasks are nothing to him.

By the words, 'love of and search for antiquity',

Confucius meant the reading of the old books, the 'Odes', and the 'Documents', the memorization of their contents, and the studying of them at the feet of a tutor. Such tasks were light for him. The word 'learning', in Confucius' time meant precisely this reading and memorization of the classics: he implies that should this be the sum total of what is entailed by learning, then it was not a very difficult discipline. But what Confucius understood by the term 'learning' did not end with this: rather these tasks were the lower limit, or the mere starting point of learning. As for the true meaning of the word for him, Confucius said, 'A man who learns without thinking is enmeshed. A man who thinks but has no learning is in a state of doubt.' If a man, that is, learns from others, and from the reading of books, and does not reflect on the meaning of his knowledge, it does not become clarified; while on the other hand, if a man merely reflects to himself, and does not study with others, he is left in a state of doubt. One should both gain one's knowledge from others, and also cull over its meaning and significance to oneself. True learning only comes with the combination of study and reflection.

Again, Confucius said, 'Hear much, and reject what is doubtful. . . . See much and exclude what is questionable.' The scope of observation and experience should be widened as far as is possible, although it is vital to reject anything that is at all questionable from this body of experience. This has much the same drift as the statement quoted previously, concerning the process which comes akin to, but still inferior to, pure knowledge: 'I hear much, and choose out the good points from what I have heard; I see much, and keep the good points in mind.' This term 'experience', which includes both visual and aural experience, covers the study of the books, such as the 'Odes' and the 'Documents', in which the civilization of early China was described in detail, and also the instructions of one's superiors, whether a tutor, or a village elder, both of which would contain a strong strain of tradition passed down from early times.

However, learning does not consist in the mere memorization of all ancient tradition without discrimination. Learning, or knowledge, is the elimination of what is ambiguous or evil from the body of ancient tradition, and the selection of what is correct and good. By these words, Confucius shows clearly that he did not unconditionally and with no reservation accept the whole body of ancient tradition, for to this, too, he applied a certain measure of critical appreciation. We must now consider the principles by which he made his selections from ancient tradition.

It was believed in Confucius' time that the two dynasties of Hsia and Yin had preceded the kingdom of Chou, and of these he said, 'I could well speak of the system of ritual of Hsia and of Yin. . . .' He did in fact frequently discuss the ritual of the two earlier dynasties, but there was no attempt or tendency to view them as a golden age, or to suggest that an ideal system of these ancient courts should be restored. Thus he exclaimed once, 'Chou had the advantage of looking back on the two previous dynasties, and what a magnificent culture it has achieved. And we—do we not follow the Chou?' There was thus no idealistic harking back to, and desire to adopt the ritual system of the two earlier dynasties: instead he sought his model in that of the Chou dynasty, a pattern near to hand.

The words cited above appear in the 'Earlier Analects', and in a section compiled very soon after Confucius' death. In the 'Later Analects', compiled at a considerably later date, to a question from Yen Hui about how to govern a state, Confucius is made to reply, 'Follow the calendar of Hsia, ride in a state carriage of Yin, and wear the ceremonial cap of Chou. In music, follow the model of the Shao Dance, banish the modes of Cheng, and keep flatterers at arm's length.' The latter part of this statement advocates the adoption of the dance set by King Wu of Chou to the music of the old sage ruler Shun, and the prohibition of the new-style music of the state of Cheng, and as a result, a statesman would be able to give a wide berth to sly and cunning flatterers. In fact, by a completely arbitrary selection of certain aspects of the regimes of the old dynasties from Shun downwards, Confucius appears to build up something like his ideal system of government. Now we must ask whether it would be true to say that Confucius did construct his own system in this way, by a careful selection from among the different regimes of the several preceding dynasties.

In point of fact, the truth is the very opposite of this. Confucius never gave way to his own personal whims, in an attempt to construct an arbitrarily chosen system on the basis of a selection from the previous dynastic regimes. This way of thinking belongs to the later Confucian scholars, widely separated in time from Confucius, who by degrees altered the nuance of these original words of Confucius. The immediate disciples, or their disciples, understood these words as meaning that since the Chou kingdom had adopted the practices of the two preceding dynasties, had combined them, and had produced from them a finely finished system, there was thus no need to hark back deliberately to the practices of the old Hsia and Yin dynasties, and seek for a model there. This is, of course, an accurate picture of the attitude of Confucius in this matter.

However, in this respect, coexistent with the comparison of the different dynastic systems, there is a hint of the idea of placing the ancient kingdoms into a historical order of development. Confucius did not overlook the process of development, although, in the 'Later Analects' he is made to appear to wish to do so. He made no attempt to stand outside this process, and return to the way of the old kingdoms, by means of an unhistorical revival of the past. Once, asked by Tzu Chang whether events of ten generations hence could be known, Confucius answered, 'In constructing its system of ritual, Yin drew from that of Hsia. In the same way, Chou borrowed from the Yin system, and any additions or rejections can be discovered. Thus the body of ritual of Chou's successor, be it even a hundred generations hence can be inferred.' Confucius thus appears as considering that from a mental grasp of the historical development of the practices of ancient kingdoms, it is possible to think out the tendency of future development, and to predict the form which the practices inaugurated by a new dynasty will take. Such a way of thinking on Confucius' part, showing him fully cognisant of the fact of development in history, was perhaps a little too advanced and progressive for his times, and there may perhaps be some doubt whether this passage does in fact record the true thought of Confucius himself.

This discussion with Tzu Chang appears in Chapter II, one of the earliest strata in the 'Analects'. However, it stands two sections before the end of its chapter, and it has been argued that at the end of each chapter there was added comparatively late material, which purported to incorporate the words of Confucius. If this be the case, this conversation of Tzu Chang with Confucius may well contain an admixture of thought of a date long posterior to the time of Confucius. However, in the words of Confucius already cited, which, we have seen, were near to the original drift of Confucius' thought, there does exist the germ of a way of thinking which is quite well aware of a process of historical development in the regimes of the earlier dynasties. Even though this latter quotation be in fact a reflection of the thought of Tzu Chang or of his school, it would be fair to say that it does more clearly reveal the historical view adopted by Confucius concerning the evolution of the administrative systems of the dynasties which preceded the Chou.

Of the more influential and important disciples who were taught in person by Confucius, Tzu Chang was the youngest, he being forty-eight years younger than Confucius. He entered the school after Confucius had returned to Lu from his journeys to the various kingdoms in northern China, and then, waiting on Confucius, he imbibed only the thoughts of the later period of his life. Thus at the base of the words of Confucius as heard and passed on by Tzu Chang, there would be a system of thought which only in a very vague and indistinct form embraced the ideas of the vital Confucius, and it would be no coincidence if this original core were pushed to, and perhaps beyond, the very margin of its legitimate limits. Yet, although the sayings of Confucius contained in the traditions of the school of Tzu Chang possess a peculiar clarity which renders them in many aspects different in tenor from the sayings recorded in the 'Earlier Analects', there is still no compelling reason for dismissing them as the accretions of later Confucian scholars.

Confucius thought then, that true knowledge consisted not in a blind acceptance of, but in a critical study of the traditions concerning the earlier dynasties. Such criticisms of tradition, and especially tradition in the form of ritual—that is, the social systems and the customs of the previous dynasties—should not be governed or swayed by personal and subjective judgments, but should be the outcome of a process of inference based on the progress of historical development, since the earliest known times, of the social practices of the Chou dynasty. Only in this way, could a critical appreciation of the trend of future developments be acquired.

Of Confucius' statement that, 'If a man enquires into the past in such a way as to acquire knowledge about the present, he is a fit person to become a teacher of others', there have been many explanations: of these, the fairest seems to be that a process of inference from a knowledge of the traditions concerning the past, brings a knowledge of present day affairs. It is not simply a matter of remembering or accepting tradition at face value: unless, running through this process of memorization, there is the additional ability to look out from this background into the future, it is of no avail. Only when a scholar has these abilities, is he qualified to become a teacher of others—and the aspiration of Confucius, himself the instructor of a large number of disciples, was this ability to learn of the present by means of an enquiry into the past.

Such was Confucius' teaching: he cannot be styled, by the usual definition of the terms, a conservative or a reactionary. We have discussed Confucius the scholar, the thinker, and the teacher. We must now turn to an examination of Confucius as statesman, for, in his younger days, he possessed an unusually intense interest in the government of his day.

FIVE

CONFUCIUS THE STATESMAN

1 'Government by Virtue.'

Confucius' political views were based on a theory of so-called 'government by means of virtue', which was the exact opposite of legalism. He said, 'If you use laws to direct the people, and punishments to control them, they will merely try to evade the laws, and will have no sense of shame. But if by virtue you guide them, and by the ritual you control them, there will be a sense of shame, and of the right.' Opposed then to the theory of rule by law—the guidance of the people by government, and coercion by the force of statutory law—was this idea of rule by means of virtue—the nurture of the people by morality, and the building of a natural order for the controlling of the people, based on the ritual. If you hedge a people round with laws, they will for ever, and with no conscience at all in the matter, be searching for loopholes in the law, and however many restrictive prohibitions are passed, it will not be possible to catch up with them. But government by virtue makes its appeal to the moral senses, and allows scope for free action; hence, illegal conduct will disappear. It was for such reasons that Confucius considered the claims of rule by virtue to be superior.

Originally, in Ch'un-ch'iu times, the government of a city-state had been in the hands of the representatives of the specific clans which comprised the state—government policy, that is, had been determined in conventions of the nobles. The normal procedure was that any dispute between clans should be settled in a consultation between the clan chiefs in conference, both sipping blood and taking an oath, invoking the name of the god, to fulfil the terms of the settlement. Transgressions which only affected members of the same clan, were entirely under the jurisdiction of the clan concerned, and so were not brought to this council for arbitration, the state thus possessing no powers of interference in such matters. The idea of government by virtue proposed by Confucius was founded on this principle of self-government within the clan, the legacy of the rule by the aristocracy of the city-state.

It was Tzu Ch'an of Cheng who first furthered the claims of legalism. In 536 B.C., he had the laws which he had enacted in Cheng engraved in the form of inscriptions on bronze vessels, and by this act, he was said to have been the first statesman in China to issue a written form of a legal code. The enactment of this written code, together with the measures for the improvement of the yield of agricultural land, and taxation reforms, formed one of the three great measures of Tzu Ch'an after his rise to the office of prime minister. Cheng, sandwiched between the two rival North and South Leagues, was obliged to pay a certain sum in tribute to each party for the preservation of her peace. It was beyond the resources of the old main clans to meet the burden of securing a revenue adequate to discharge this obligation, so Tzu Ch'an relaxed the property restrictions on the holding of agricultural land by the general people, and inaugurated a plan to increase its productive power. There was no machinery within the framework of the old clan council for levying taxes on the general people—for they stood outside of the sphere of the autonomous authority of the main clans. There was a serious need for a new statute applicable to the people who did not belong to any such organization, to make it possible to ensure, and if necessary enforce, payment of tax by them to the state treasury. Tzu Ch'an's proclamation of a written code of law was both the outcome of the peculiar international situation in which Cheng found herself placed, and again the consequence of his economic measures.

However, twenty-three years after Cheng had promulgated a written code, she was followed by the leader of the Northern League, Tsin, who in 513 B.C., inscribed her statutes on bronze vessels. In Tsin, the need for a new written code arose in consequence of the passing of new taxation regulations to support the development of the military budget of the state. Here again, as was the case with Cheng, the codification of the law was achieved in concomitance with new taxation regulations. Confucius was forty years of age at this time, and was just beginning to formulate his own political philosophy.

In the Tso Commentary, there is an account of Confucius' reaction on hearing the report of this enactment of the codification of the law in Tsin: he vehemently criticised Tsin for rejecting the legal system of Duke Wen, famous in the central plain as one of the first leaders of the leagued states, and for adopting a new codified law. Whether these are or are not the words of Confucius, it is difficult now to establish, although as the Confucius of the 'Analects' denounces legalism, and adopts the theory of government by virtue, he must indeed have felt very strongly about any such report connected with a matter so important in the sphere of government.

The head state of the north, Tsin, had followed Cheng in the publication of a written law code, and the enactment of such a written code had developed into a new fashion in most of the states of the plain in the later years of the Ch'un-ch'iu period. Against this sudden rise of legalism, and the definite trend of the times in these years, Confucius took a firm stand, and politically at least, he should perhaps be regarded as very much the conservative and the reactionary. As has been noted before, the basis of his ideal of government by virtue lay in the autonomy and independence of the main clans forming the city-state. Now in recent years, the influence of the old nobles had gradually weakened, and their clans also were by degrees disintegrating as power groups, so that in place of the old independent clan system, there was a demand for the new written law as a means of strengthening the political organization of the state community. The question we must now ask is whether Confucius did in fact turn his back completely on the trends of his times.

In terms of power and influence, the state of Lu, where Confucius was born, was far inferior to the head-states of both the leagues, Tsin and Ch'u, and again to Ch'i, her neighbour, and the former leader of the northern alliance. Lu's territory lay in the modern Shantung, far to the east from the central plain, and she was, culturally speaking, very undeveloped, and quite unable to compare with such kingdoms as Cheng and Wei, the cultural hub of the central plain. The boast that Lu was the state which had come into the inheritance of the true tradition of the Duke of Chou was perhaps a creation of the time, posterior to Confucius himself, when Confucianism flourished there. There is not the slightest doubt but that culturally as well as in terms of influence, Lu was backward, and this backwardness may have been a latent cause for the conservatism, or the reactionary nature of Confucius' political theory.

However, on this point, it should be noted that there

are essential points of difference between the old-style 'government by virtue', built on the framework of the concept of the independence of the clan within the state, and the new version as advocated by Confucius. One of the most potent factors in the independence of the clan was the strength of the degree of unity and solidarity within it, and the clan member could not set himself up as an entity separate and independent from the clan, or assert any degree of individuality. Members of the clan were under the permanent restraint of this solidarity of the clan, and led a real and active life only in so far as they were regarded as members of the clan group: the liberty of the individual was in this respect markedly limited, and there was an unconscious submission to the regulations of the group.

In complete contrast, Confucius' 'government by virtue' was built on the conscience of the individual, for the moral awakening of the individual is regarded as its foundation. In the case also of the ruler, in Confucius' words, 'When his person is correct, matters will proceed with no need of commands: but when his person is incorrect, he may issue commands, but the people will not obey them.' Thus if there is no lofty moral character inherent in the statesman who gives the orders, it cannot be expected that his orders will secure the obedience of the people. Government would be carried out most perfectly in a situation in which both ruler and ruled were persons of good character, and were together possessed of a moral awareness. There is a further statement of the ideal, 'He who brought virtue to the task of government could be likened to the North Star, fixed in its constant place, with all the constellations clustered round it.'

In this way, with a mutual understanding between prince and servant, government can be conducted in complete and unobstructed harmony. Asked by Duke Ching of Ch'i about the secret of good government, Confucius answered, 'It consists in the prince being prince, the servant being servant, father being father, and son being son.' If the prince properly discharges his part as prince, then the servant will fulfil his own due functions. The most important requisite for good government, as Confucius taught, was this mutual discharge of respective duties, as dictated by the individual's moral conscience. Confucius replied in much the same vein to a question by Duke Ting of Lu, about the principles which should govern a ruler's treatment of his ministers, and the ministers' service to their prince: 'The prince should treat his minister in conformity with the dictates of ritual, and the minister's service of his prince should be always loyal and faithful.' That is, the discharge of one's function should result in action which conforms with the canons of ritual, and in this respect, the standard is the ritual which grows from and conforms to the custom of the group. However, convention, even though it be not set down in writing and transformed into a written codified law, is after all, a kind of law, and thus, while Confucius attacked only the recent introduction of a written law, he does not seem to have reached the point of realization that the convention of the state, of the clan, of the household, and so on, is in fact a form of law. Confucius thought that action in accordance with the law should not be unconscious, but should stem from the realization by the individual of his proper place and function within a group, and should be an autonomous obedience, as to a moral imperative. Herein, there lies the basic difference from the concept of the nature of the law prevailing under the old-time government by virtue. Confucius was not opposed to the law itself: it would be more correct to argue that he expected that results similar to those obtainable by the working of the law could be gained autonomously through the moral awakening of the individual.

Confucius' political theory of 'government by virtue' was opposed to the legalist theories prevalent in his day: nevertheless, it would be wrong to regard it as in entirety a theory opposed and running contrary to the age, and to criticise it on such grounds. Born into an age when the original autonomy of the clan within the state had decayed and was lost, Confucius ventured to advocate a theory of government by virtue, of which the central idea was based on this very clan autonomy of earlier times. But the structure of this ideal government by virtue was built on the foundation not of the group consciousness of the clan, but on the moral awareness of the individual. In freeing politics from the influence of the group consciousness of the clan, and in postulating that it should be a matter for the moral consciousness of the individual, freed from and rendered independent of the control of the clan, Confucius can hardly be said to have been more of a progressive than the legalist theoreticians of his day, who laid great emphasis on the idea of national consciousness, but at least he is to be ranked with the latter as being one of the influential political thinkers of his time.

2 *Opposition to the Oligarchy of the 'Three Huan'*

In the adoption and consolidation of his individual political standpoint, Confucius showed that he was of no mean ability in turning to advantage the prevailing state of affairs. As an active statesman, he was no opportunist, bending and submitting to powers too strong for him, or riding with the times: instead, he was an idealist who did not know the meaning of deviation from the way indicated by his own convinced and firmly held beliefs.

Government should be rooted on the moral consciousness of man. Thus the secret of government lay in the appointment of men of high moral character as statesmen. Asked by Duke Ai of Lu how best to secure the submission of the people, Confucius answered, 'Elevate the straight: if you impose them on the crooked, the people will submit: elevate the crooked and impose them on the straight, and there will be no submission.' These words are explained as a thinly veiled criticism of Duke Ai's government, for he did not place honest and morally upright men in high office, but governed through wicked and dishonest ministers. From Confucius' point of view, at least, crooked (that is, dishonest and iniquitous) retainers controlled the government of Lu. But, to clarify this statement, we should examine, in closer detail, the state of the Lu government at this time.

As I have said in Chapter I, in the later part of the Ch'un-ch'iu period, at about the time of the birth of Confucius, the influence of the three families, Meng-sun, Shu-sun, and Chi-sun, descended from an earlier prince of Lu, Duke Huan, had become extremely wide and powerful. They had grasped complete political power, and there ruled, in fact, an oligarchy of the three families, the 'Three Huan'. The most influential of the three was the Chi-sun family. The three had made hereditary prerogatives of the various more important offices of the Lu government, although there had grown the convention that the position of premier was filled until his death by the eldest of the chiefs of the three households. At the period when Confucius was reaching mature years, the office was filled, in virtue of his seniority, by Chao-tzu, of the Shu-sun family. On the other hand, the real power wielded by the Chi family was such that the Chi was able alone to confront the

Shu-sun and Meng-sun families, and its chieftain, Chi P'ing-tzu did exercise a *de facto* domination over the government of Lu.

When Confucius was thirty-six (in 517 B.C.), Duke Chao, the prince of Lu, conducted celebrations in honour of his predecessor Duke Hsiang. Dances and music were to be performed at Duke Hsiang's ancestral temple, but such was the utter poverty and decay into which the court had fallen, that it was unable to maintain the requisite group of specialist musicians and dancers. Although this was a formal celebration in honour of the state ancestors, only two dancers were able to turn out, and they could only present a very ragged and ill-sorted dance. As against this, at the festival held in the household temple of the Chi family, there was a performance of a dance, with music, with eight rows of performers, and each row containing eight members, the dancers thus being sixty-four in number. When he saw this, Confucius exclaimed in indignation, 'Having eight rows of dancers in his hall! He who does not shame to do this, would not be ashamed of anything.'

A dance with eight rows of performers, sixty-four in all, was part of the highly formal ceremony permitted only to the Chou royal house. The Chi family—arrière-vassals from the standpoint of the Chou Emperor—used this dance in its own household celebrations to its family ancestors, and such presumptuous behaviour on the part of the completely unqualified Chi family in the court of the weakened Lu prince, would be viewed with anger and chagrin by the young Confucius. But not everyone in Lu looked on idly at the eclipse of the fortunes of the princely house of Lu and the tyranny of the 'Three Huan'; Confucius was not the only one to be incensed at this sight which was more than the eye could bear, for the Prince of Lu also was finally goaded into action.

The reign of this prince, Duke Chao, at the end of the middle years of the Ch'un-ch'iu period, coincided with an age in which there occurred frequent murders or expulsions of the rulers of the group of states of the central plain. Although disputes concerning the succession to the throne of the various states were by no means rare occurrences in the early part of the Ch'un-ch'iu period, there was a clear distinguishing factor between the disorders of the early and of the middle periods. Civil disturbances of the early period arose from quarrels between factions of nobles attempting to wrest power from a powerful and despotic prince. Those of the middle period were part of a last trial of strength on the part of the princes, now rendered ineffective in the sphere of government, in opposition to the nobles, who had by now made all high offices their hereditary privilege, and who were by degrees usurping the entire authority of the princes.

The state rulers could not acquiesce in such treatment from the nobles, and strengthened their resolve to overthrow the oligarchic regime which the nobles had built. The political and social conditions of the times made it possible for the rulers to entertain hopes of this nature, for from about this juncture, there began to take place a remarkable change in the power-distribution of the social classes of the city-states, and the social authority wielded by the noble classes themselves started to disintegrate. There was a gradual trend towards a transfer of power to the newly constituted class of knights whose members were gaining wisdom and military prowess, and who, by virtue of these talents, had gone into the service of the noble families. The princes planned, by appointing to office such military knights or bureaucrats, who had but recently come to prominence, at a single coup to snatch away the monopoly of the government from the hands of the old noble cliques.

The time is the year 530 B.C., thirteen years before the occasion of the staging of the eight rows' dance by the Chi family which incurred the wrath of Confucius. P'ing-tzu, who had succeeded to the position of elder of the Chi family, had omitted to send greetings, on the occasion of his accession, to Nan K'uai, who was the mayor of the town of Pi, the fortified headquarters of the Chi family. Harbouring dissatisfaction at this slight, Nan K'uai plotted to drive out P'ing-tzu, and to return the fief and the wealth of the Chi household to the state of Lu. Unfortunately, however, the secret plan failed, and unsuccessful in a further attempt to surrender his town of Pi to the neighbouring state of Ch'i, he fled in the end to Ch'i. Thus, governmental authority, which had before passed from the hands of the princes to the nobles, now again at this juncture, passed to the hands of men of the new class of knights, the retainers of the nobles. The old story of the inferior turning against and vanquishing his superior was retold in the events in Lu at the time of Confucius' growth to manhood, at the close of the middle period of the Ch'un-ch'iu era.

While P'ing-tzu was staging his dance of the eight rows (a usurpation of the ritual permitted solely to the Chou Emperor) in his great festival at the family shrine, and was giving himself up to grandiose and extravagant dreams, a plot to overthrow in one move the autocratic authority of the Chi house was being worked out in strict secrecy. The seed of the conflict lay in a quarrel between P'ing-tzu and his near neighbours the Hou family. Again, the fact that the Chi had harboured one Tsang Tseng after his flight as a result of an internal clan dispute within the Tsang family was the starting point of mutual hostility between the Chi and the Tsang. The Tsang family was the most illustrious clan in Lu, and had produced many wise and famous statesmen: hitherto, it had for generations maintained the closest of relations with the Chi family.

P'ing-tzu's grandfather and great-grandfather had both capably and with great credit filled the office of premier of Lu, and P'ing-tzu himself maintained close relations with some of the high officials of the state of Tsin, the leader of the northern league. Thus his influence both in external and internal affairs of state was strongly backed, and relying on the authority of his house, he shamelessly staged this dance. The brazen usurpation caused a frown on the faces of all men of goodwill. However, though inferior in terms of power to the 'Three Huan', the Tsang family yet enjoyed a certain degree of acknowledged prestige in Lu; in the eyes of the rest of the disaffected young bloods of the nobility, to have fallen foul of this distinguished clan had disclosed a gap now too wide to be bridged.

One day in the ninth month of the year 517 B.C., Shu-sun Chao-tzu, who had gained the confidence of the people of Lu for his efficient handling of his office as prime minister, was out in the country. Seizing upon this opportunity, the disaffected young noblemen leagued with the Hou clan, and raised a force which stormed and invaded the country seat which belonged to the Chi clan. Caught off his guard, P'ing-tzu fled to a tower standing at one corner of the battlements. There, negotiations were begun with the young noblemen who had gathered and laid siege to him. The Chi chieftain begged to be allowed to retire to the suburbs of the city, but the plea was not accepted: he then offered conditions whereby he would resign his ministerial rank, and would retire to his town of Pi, but these also were disallowed. Immediately he proposed that he should load the family wealth on to five chariots, and leave the state, but this in turn was turned down. It seemed that on no account was Chi P'ing-tzu to be allowed to escape from this predicament with his life.

In fact, if at this juncture some compromise could have been reached, and the Chi chieftain quietly had been sent off either to the country, or to some foreign state, the plan of the Duke could have been brought to complete fruition. A far-sighted loyal retainer, by the name of Tzu Chia-tzu was incessantly suggesting terms on which the dispute might be settled, but the Duke refused unconditionally to agree to such terms. In the meanwhile, an old retainer of the Shu-sun family who had been left in command during the absence of his lord, had gathered the members of his household, and began to address them, 'We are retainers. We do not presume to know anything of the interests of the state as a whole. Which is the better for us, that the Lord of the Chi live or die?' In these words, he reminded his audience that they were the servants not of the Duke of Lu, but of the Shu-sun family. As such, the affairs of the Shu-sun house were of much greater import to them than those of the state. This being the case, if the Chi house were to fall, and the Duke were once again to grasp in his own hands the reins of government, what would be the general effect on the Shu-sun family, and, of course, on their livelihood as that family's servants?

'If the Chi Lord perish, that marks the end of the Shu-sun Lord also', was the immediate reply from every mouth. That is, the interests of the Chi and the Shu-sun clans were by and large identical. Thus help should be sent to the Chi clan. The decision was unanimous, and troops were levied immediately to form a force to be sent to the rescue of P'ing-tzu, and the Meng-sun clan as well lost no time in adding a unit to the relieving army. Confronted by the combined force of the seasoned troops of these two households, the motley units of the army under the Duke of Lu offered little resistance and were thoroughly routed.

Thus the coup d'état of Duke Chao, which for an instant had seemed destined for success, failed within the day. Duke Chao fled for his life from the capital, and was obliged to retire to Ch'i, where he lived for seven years in exile until his death. It would be said that the 'Three Huan' were acting the tyrant in Lu, but, fortunately, from one aspect at least, the much weakened ducal house, completely shorn of any influence in the conduct of the government, was content to act as their lackey, so that, as far as could be seen by the other states, there was no disorder in the matter of the succession to the throne. Still more important, there were no bloody and cruel murders of princes by the noble families in power. This was the first occasion in the long history of Lu that her Duke had met with the opposition of his people, and had been expelled from his realm.

It was in the same year that the young Confucius had boiled over in righteous indignation at the staging of the eight-row dance in the forecourt of the Chi house. There is little need to waste words in a description of the feelings with which Confucius would have looked on this usurpation of the regal prerogatives. But there is complete silence in the historical documents of Lu, and no statement remains to us which refers to any action which Confucius, still obscure at this time, was led to take.

Confucius once said, 'Though the barbarians to our east and north possess princes, they still cannot rank with the states of China who do not.' (There is, and has been certain conflict over the precise translation and interpretation of this verse: Chu Hsi, 1130-1200, the great Sung dynasty orthodox interpreter of the Classics adopts what is from a grammatical point of view, the somewhat forced interpretation, 'If rulers were to be established even among the tribes of the east and north, they would still not be like the states of China proper who have no ruler.') However, the point to note lies in the final words concerning the interpretation of which there is no dispute: the words 'who have no ruler' must have been intended as a concrete and pointed reference to Confucius' own state of Lu, which suffered a long period of seven years' interregnum after the flight of Duke Chao to Ch'i.

After the enforced flight of Duke Chao, Chi P'ing-tzu held his throne as regent, and as he took to wearing the ornamental jewel of office, rightfully that of the Duke, the question even arose whether P'ing-tzu, on his death, should be buried wearing the jewel. Now what would be Confucius' reaction on seeing this state of affairs? How could he acquiesce in this complacent usurpation of the vacant throne of Lu by P'ing-tzu? Again, what about the very fact of the vacant throne? Doubts began to occur in Confucius' mind whether, since even the barbarians were said to possess rulers, the administration of their states might not be superior to that of Lu. These were misgivings not to be repressed: thus there were perhaps stirrings of the notion that he would rather fly from Lu, cut himself off from the central states, and go off to the kingdoms of the bar-barians. Yet, on the other side of the picture, the king-doms of the centre were, after all, the home of culture: Lu's prince had been forced from his state, but Lu was, in the end, the birth-place of Confucius. In the final analysis, the conclusion to which he came was that he ought perhaps to remain in Lu, and in the confines of

China proper—but that he should set himself to re-model Lu, and improve the conditions of China.

Yet this high-handed tyranny of P'ing-tzu of Chi was unbearable: he could not bring himself to live even for a day in a Lu of this kind—and he did at one juncture feel a strong urge to get in a boat, and sail away to the lands of the barbarians. The 'Analects' contains no clear record of the date of this impulse, although there are references to the fact of Confucius visiting the state of Ch'i, conversing with its prince, Duke Ching, and listening to the famous music of Ch'i. Ssu-ma Ch'ien, the author of the 'Historical Records' correctly interpreted Confucius' departure for Ch'i as the outcome of the internal disorder consequent on Duke Chao's flight from his country, and it thus appears that Confucius followed his ruler, Duke Chao, to his place of exile in Ch'i.

3 Visit to Ch'i, and the Formation of Confucius' Group of Scholars

Although we may be reasonably sure that Confucius followed Duke Chao in the latter's flight to Ch'i in 517 B.C., there is no evidence by which to determine the length of his stay in Ch'i. This was Confucius' first trip abroad, and his experiences must undoubtedly have left many vivid impressions on his mind—susceptible and receptive as it would have been at the age of thirty-six. As has been stated above, Lu was a small state, tucked away in the eastern edge of the central plain. Ch'i had long before provided one of the most outstanding leaders of the northern confederacy, in her Duke Huan, and at this period, her capital, which had taken immense strides in commercial and industrial development, contended for first place as the largest metropolis of the Chinese world. When Confucius, the country bumpkin, first set foot in this capital, Lin-tse, there would be many new sights and sounds, all of a kind to evoke wonder and fascination.

While he was in Ch'i, Confucius heard the Shao music, said to be the composition of Shun, the Emperor of olden times. Instantly charmed by it, he went forthwith to the college of musicians, and for three months forgetting sleep and food, he devoted himself completely to his lessons. This episode is recorded in a verse of the 'Analects' in the words, 'The Master heard the Shao music in Ch'i, and for three months he did not know the taste of meat', and Confucius is elsewhere recorded as saying, 'I did not reckon that the beauty of music could reach such a pitch.' It seems that in addition to the fact that the airs of the music studied by Confucius under the Music Master of Lu were old-fashioned, their performance by an impoverished orchestral group was a somewhat mean and squalid one. In complete contrast, the performance by a full orchestra of hand-picked musical specialists attached to the court of a leading and influential state carried away completely its receptive hearer.

There is also little doubt that Confucius would have heard a great deal of the achievements of the famous premier Kuan Chung, the much vaunted hero of Ch'i. The whole façade of the urban culture of Ch'i's metropolis would move the spirit of the young Confucius. However, this Confucius, strong of will, and for ever examining himself, would presently awake from this dream of enchantment by such a florid civilization; there are slight indications of a reconsideration of the power to charm the senses in the music which had for three whole months stolen his mind and body.

Kuan Chung's defence against the inroads of the eastern and southern barbarian tribes, and his fight for the civilization of the central states were indeed noble achievements. Yet, feeling that Kuan Chung's conduct —at least if the traditions told by the men of Ch'i were true to fact—did not spring from a complete personality, Confucius even went so far as to pass judgment on him in the words, 'Kuan Chung's talents were indeed minor, were they not?' Finally, he spoke his mind with the words, 'Ch'i, by one change, could reach to Lu's standard: Lu, by a single alteration, would reach the Way.' The florid civilization of Ch'i, and the unpretending culture of Lu were not noticeably of a different nature, and both civilizations were basically bound up with the Way—the way of life of which the Duke of Chou was the founder. That of Ch'i had suffered perhaps too much change and modernization, but with a slight rectification, it would become identical with that of Lu, and the latter, after small amendments, could be restored to the original pattern—the creation of the Duke of Chou. After his earlier rejection of Lu's culture and the adoption of that of Ch'i, Confucius gradually turned back towards an appreciation and re-estimation of the worth of the culture of his native state.

There was a deep-seated reason at the back of Confucius' decision to give up Ch'i's way of life and return to Lu. He had gone to Ch'i on the heels of, and perhaps largely because of his respect for his prince Duke Chao, driven from his native state, and refusing to have anything more to do with the oligarchy of the 'Three Huan'. Now it is to be conjectured that as soon as he gave the matter any close consideration, Confucius soon came to realize that the internal situation in Ch'i, far from being largely the same as that in Lu, was far worse. The influential families of Ch'i, in the middle years of the Ch'un-ch'iu period, were the Ts'ui, the Ch'ing, and the T'ien. At first, the influence of the Ts'ui family had been the greatest, but angered at his wife's illicit intrigues with Duke Chuang of Ch'i, the family head of the time, in 548 B.C., had been driven in the end to murder the Duke. This was an event which took place thirty years before the arrival of Confucius in Ch'i in 517 B.C.; however, informed of the details of the affair, though it concerned an earlier ruler of a kingdom not his own, he must still have deplored an occasion which, compared with the exile of his own country's prince, seemed much more ignoble and disgraceful.

However, the Ts'ui family was soon made to pay retribution for this atrocity. With the Ch'ing family, the Ts'ui supported Duke Ching for the vacant throne, and, supplying their nominees for the offices of Minister of the Right and Left, the two together arbitrarily controlled the government of Ch'i. But there was an immediate rift between them, and finally, attacked by the Ch'ing family, the Ts'ui household was completely wiped out. The Ch'ings then took sole control over the office of premier, and surrendered themselves to a life of complete debauchery, spending their time drinking and hunting. Soon, internal disorders within the family were the signal for other noble families, led by the T'ien, to join forces and attack the Ch'ing, who were defeated and obliged to flee far to the south, to the state of Wu.

With the influence of the Ts'ui and the Ch'ing thus entirely eradicated, the way lay clear for a rapid rise on the part of the T'ien family, which had only recently come to the fore. The intelligent chieftain of the T'ien house did not wish to vaunt the influential position which his family had achieved, but schemed to work in harmony with the old noble houses of Ch'i, and secured the advancement of a popular and able administrator in Yén Tzu, who was given the office of premier: in actual fact, behind this figurehead, the real power and influence in the kingdom was gradually being amassed by the leader of the T'ien house, who soon possessed sufficient hidden authority to be able to act as if the state were without a ruler, or to be able to kill or drive out that ruler. Confucius, who had been unable to bring himself to witness the tyrannic administration of the 'Three Huan', and had followed his ruler, Duke Chao, into exile to Ch'i, was now compelled to watch helplessly the savage despotism of the T'ien family in Ch'i; in fact the crisis with which the latter menaced the ducal house was far more threatening than anything which the 'Three Huan' might have offered to the prince of Lu.

Sorrowful and disillusioned by conditions in Ch'i, Confucius presently departed, and returned to Lu. The date of his return, as I have stated above, cannot be proved, but it is to be surmised that it was around the year 509 B.C., when, on the death of Duke Chao in disillusion in a town near the frontier of Ch'i, the accession of his younger brother Duke Ting brought an end to the long period of the interregnum. Confucius would have been about forty years of age by this time. In later life, as he recollected the past, he said of himself, 'At forty, I had no doubts'. Through the experiences gained in foreign travel, his field of vision had been broadened, and he had arrived at the point at which he could formulate an individual and independent attitude, with a firm confidence in his abilities, and a knowledge of his weaknesses.

It is said that about ten years before this, Meng Hsi-tzu a member of one of the 'Three Huan' families, had left an injunction to the elder of the family on his death, that his sons Meng I-tzu and Nan-kung Ching-shu should take lessons in ritual from Confucius. It was perhaps from about this time that disciples began to come in some number to Confucius, attracted by his

145

scholastic and moral qualities. To judge from the ages of the more important disciples as they are given in the 'Historical Records', if we calculate for the moment the date of Confucius' return to Lu as 509 B.C., the eldest disciple, Tzu Lu, was thirty-five in that year, Min-tzu was twenty-nine, Jan Po-niu was twenty-seven, and Yu Jo twenty-one. Thus, as these disciples were all of quite mature years at this time, it seems reasonable to assume that they entered the school soon after Confucius' return from Ch'i, and that the academic group centred on Confucius had begun to gather, at the latest, immediately after the return to Lu.

'I have never refused to give instruction to anyone —even the man who brings with him only his bundle of dried flesh.' A bundle of dried flesh was the ritual sign of entry into a school, and Confucius here states his habit of giving instruction in person to all who came to him in this way. Of his educational methods, he says: 'If a student is not eager, I do not begin to open up the subject for him: if he is not able to state his own views, I do not help him out. When I have disclosed one part of a topic to him, if he does not come back to me having himself worked out the other three, I do not trouble to see him again.' Confucius never forced his teaching on any of his pupils unless the pupil had first sought the Way, and, in his inability to find it, had become irritated at heart, and was growing impatient in his requests for an explanation.

The aim was so to handle a student that he spontaneously posed problems, and in giving an answer to such problems, Confucius would do no more than hint at the general outline of the solution: the student was expected to work out the remaining details of the answer by his own thought-processes. There was no detailed explanation of the problem posed, and students who could not by their own mental efforts gain an understanding of the complete solution of the problem, from the guidance and the pointers given by the Master, were not invited to return for further tuition. This was, indeed, developmental education in its most literal sense.

This educational method, so completely different from that of teachers before him, who had tried merely to inculcate some knowledge of the 'Odes' and the 'Documents' and have ancient tradition committed to memory, would not fail to draw on Confucius the attention of the people of his times. Consequently, there was a gradual increase in the number of the disciples. In fact, seventy-seven (the so-called 'Seventy') are known by name, and of these, more than half were citizens of Lu, there being comparatively few who came from the surrounding kingdoms. The disciples who joined the school at the outset, or in the very early stages of its growth, such as Tzu Lu, Min-tzu, Jan Po-niu, were of Lu origin, for at the time of the foundation of the school, Confucius' reputation as a scholar was confined to the boundaries of his own state. Again, there were only two of the students who came from the noble classes, Nan-kung Ching-shu, mention of whom has already been made above, and one Ssu-ma Niu of Sung, who joined the school later. Of the rest, the majority came, as did their Master, from the rising class of knights. The object of many of this class of student was to use the learning acquired in the course of their education in the service either of the state or of some influential noble family. To pupils who sought such advancement in office, Confucius gave not merely a vocational training, or skill in applied learning. The first principle and the main aim of his teaching was the nurture of character, and the inculcation of a basic knowledge which would fit a man to act in the way of an ideal human being.

4 *Confucius the Would-be Revolutionary*

The seven year period following the expulsion of Duke Chao to Ch'i during which P'ing-tzu, as head of the Chi family, completely controlled Lu, marked the apex of the power of the 'Three Huan'. But it is ironical that it was during this period that there were sown the seeds of the plot to undermine the authority of the Chi family and its partners. Power had passed to the Chi family retainers—drawn from the new class of knights —and there occurred a revolt of these retainers.

On the death of P'ing-tzu in 505 B.C., Yang Hu, who was the head retainer to the household, proposed that the precious state jewel of Lu, which P'ing-tzu had worn during his tenure of the regency, should be placed inside his coffin and interred with him. Another family servant, Chung-liang Huai, in whose care the jewel was placed, steadfastly refused to countenance this high-handed proposition, and from this difference of opinion concerning the funeral rites, a feud grew which split the Chi family into two factions, the Yang Hu group, and the opposition. There was much confusion, and this buccaneer Yang Hu seized every member of the clan, including even Huan-tzu, who had succeeded P'ing-tzu as head of the clan, and who would on no account entertain Yang Hu's proposals. The whole group was dragged off to an open square in front of the southern gate of the metropolis of Lu, and there forced on oath to agree to the expulsion of the leader of the opposing faction, Kung-fu Wen-po, the most popular member of the entire clan, along with other less distinguished members.

Having succeeded in bending the whole Chi clan to his will, Yang Hu began to amass in his own hands the means to authority in Lu, in place of Huan-tzu of the Chi. The 'Three Huan', who, up to this point, had dictated to the prince, and had monopolized the government, were now in turn forced to go on their knees to Yang Hu, and became his obedient tools. The oligarchy of the 'Three Huan' gave way to the despotism of the upstart Yang Hu, but recently the Chi clan retainer, and for three years he held complete control of Lu. But, as is often the case with men unaccustomed and new to power, that power was abused, and Yang Hu became over-presumptuous. He won over the disaffected group of the Chi clan and the Shu-sun clan, together with the retainers and servants of both, put to death those of the chief members of the 'Three Huan' clans for whom he felt any personal dislike, and plotted to bring them all over to his faction.

One day in October, Yang Hu summoned Huan-tzu of the Chi family, with the pretext of offering sacrifice to the founder of Lu. The real intent was to murder Huan-tzu in the courtyard where the sacrifice was to take place, and to this end, Yang Hu had, on the previous day, issued a proclamation for the mobilization of all war-chariots in the Lu capital, Ch'ü-fou. Suspecting something untoward, the head of the Meng-sun family had advised his colleagues to be on their guard, but, on the day in question, Yang Yüeh, a cousin of Yang Hu, called for Huan-tzu and putting him in a carriage, began to drive towards the ground where the ceremony was to be held. During the drive, Huan-tzu won over the personal coachman to the Yang family, Lin Ch'u, and had him instantly swerve from the road, and make off in the direction of the house of the Meng family. Yang Yüeh was forthwith killed as a scapegoat, and a violent street-battle broke out between the warriors loyal to the Meng household, and the troops of Yang Hu. The battle was decided by the arrival at the capital of a large force from the base fort of the Meng clan, and Yang Hu made his way into the palace of the Duke of Lu, stripped off his armour, and donned civilian clothing. He stole the precious jewel and large ceremonial bow which were stored in the palace for safe keeping, as being hereditary state treasures, and after spending one night leisurely in the city suburbs, he escaped across the border on the following day, and made his way to the state of Ch'i.

Confucius was very probably living in the capital of Lu at this time, and may well have experienced at first hand the savagery of Yang Hu's dictatorship. What attitude would he have adopted towards this dictatorship in his years of discretion? (He was now, according to the chronology we have proposed to follow, aged fifty.) There does in fact remain to us a single section of the 'Analects' which has reference to Confucius' dealings with Yang Hu. This section has become something of a crux for the commentators on the 'Analects' and the biographers of Confucius. The episode is contained in the first verse of Chap. XVII, and the whole chapter takes its name of 'Yang Huo' from this first section and the first words of the section. The verse reads, 'Yang Huo wished to see Confucius, but Confucius refused to appear at an interview. Yang Huo thereupon sent Confucius a present of a pig, and Confucius waited until a time when he knew that Yang Huo was not at home to pay his visit of thanks. However, the two met accidentally on the street.' Yang Huo then wished to have Confucius accept office, and sought to arrange to see him in person, but Confucius would not appear. Yang Huo then sent an emissary with the gift of a pig, to the residence of Confucius, and hoped to catch him, and persuade him into office when he called to render thanks for the gift. But Confucius saw through the underlying motive, and so as to avoid meeting with Yang Huo, chose a time when the latter was not at home for the return visit. But when the two met accidentally in the street, Yang Huo faced Confucius and said to him, 'Come! I wish to speak with you. Could it be called an act of "humanity" to possess a valuable jewel such as you have, and cheat your state of it?' By this, Yang Huo meant that when one possessed the genius of Confucius, he could not be styled loyal to the community if he refused to serve it: such refusal would engender misgivings on the part of the populace, and could not be termed 'humanity'. To this question, Confucius replied, 'No, it cannot.' Yang Huo went on to ask, 'Can one who, in spite of a desire to serve in office, is for ever failing to grasp his opportunities, be called a wise man?' This was a hint at Confucius' trip abroad to Ch'i, and his failure to turn the times to his advantage in his various attempts to influence political matters. Confucius agreed that such conduct could not be defined as wisdom, whereupon Yang Huo went on, 'Time is slipping by. The years will not stop for us.'— Yang Huo wished Confucius to accept office, and to come forward during his own lifetime, and at the time of his tenure of the office of premier of Lu. To this statement, Confucius' reply was, 'Very well: I will accept office.'—in the end, against his original intentions, he was unable to resist Yang Huo's importunity, and finally consented to serve under him.

The early commentators on the text of the 'Analects' believed that Yang Huo was another name for Yang Hu. If their interpretation is correct, then Confucius bent the knee to the upstart Chi family retainer, and agreed to serve as an official under his savage dictatorship. However, to orthodox scholars, that a personality the like of Confucius, who had so strongly attacked the arrogant administration of the 'Three Huan', and especially that of the Chi clan, should so ignobly consent to work under the direction of a villain the like of Yang Hu, could not be accepted as fact, and scholars of this mind tried to argue that Yang Huo and Yang Hu were not identical.

In spite of such attempts to save Confucius, the early pronunciation of the characters written for Huo and Hu is phonetically very close, and it seems that the personal name of Yang Hu was also pronounced Huo in dialect. Further, the manner of speech of this Yang Huo is in all aspects very much that of a man who had grasped the governmental authority of Lu, and he is clearly the *de facto* ruler. Of the Lu statesmen of Confucius' time, it is not to be imagined that there would be a member of the Yang family other than Yang Hu who would be capable of uttering words such as these. There can hardly be room for the slightest doubt that the original compiler of this chapter of the 'Analects' included this story fully conscious of the fact that this Yang Huo, and the Yang Hu who appeared as the despot of Lu in the Tso Commentary and in other historical records, were one and the same person.

On the other hand, there remains the problem that the 'Yang Huo' Chapter of the 'Analects' (Chapter XVII), forms a part of the section compiled at a very late date. Thus, the story of Confucius unconcernedly agreeing to go into the service of such an upstart is liable to suspicion as being perhaps a fabrication thought up by very much later Confucian scholars.

Bearing in mind such doubts in connection with Chapter XVII, we must turn to another section of the same chapter which tells of the summoning of Confucius by one Kung-shan Fu-jao who, as local resident, governed the home stronghold of Pi for the Chi clan, and who was at the time contemplating raising the standard of revolt from the Chi clan. Confucius at once replied that he would go and obey the summons, and, detained by Tzu Lu, to whom it seemed that Confucius' conduct revealed a certain disregard of the true relation which should obtain between ruler and subject, he replied, 'Need this invitation to me be entirely in vain? If he were to employ me, might I not make an "Eastern Chou" of his kingdom?' This passage again cannot be satisfactorily interpreted in any other way than that Confucius was perfectly prepared to go and serve under a Chi clan retainer. In just the same way as, at the fall of West Chou, a Chou had been re-established in the east at Lo-yang, so Confucius himself now began to see the vision of building another 'Eastern Chou' in Lu of the East, and of reviving the now moribund Way of the Chou royal court—and of achieving this ideal through the agency of Kung-shan Fu-jao.

This same Chapter XVII contains a further reference to a retainer of the Chao family (the most influential among the great families who monopolized high office in the state of Tsin) by name Fu Hsi, the Keeper of the Castle of Chung-mou. Rebelling against his lords, the Chao family, and plotting to return the fort which he governed to the kingdom of Wei, he wished to engage Confucius as one of his political advisers. Confucius was minded to go to Chung-mou forthwith, but again it was Tzu Lu who indignantly remonstrated with him; the exchange of views on the propriety of this action is recorded here.

There are thus three similar situations. In the first, albeit reluctantly and against his immediate reaction, Confucius was inclined to go into the service of Yang Hu, the Chi family retainer who was in revolt against his influential family. Secondly, he intended to comply with the invitation from Kung-shan Fu-jao, a servant of the same Chi family, who had revolted in possession of the fort of Pi and was fighting against his employers: and, thirdly, Confucius was willing to accept the invitation of Fu Hsi, an official in the service of the illustrious Chao family of Tsin, in revolt against his overlord. In all three instances, Confucius was summoned by the forces of revolt, and in each case the revolt was that of a retainer of a powerful clan, which, in the different kingdoms, was at the head of a close oligarchy. It was to such movements then that Confucius was prepared to lend his support.

As the retainer was a family servant who had sworn allegiance to the head of the family he served, he had only an indirect relation with the ruler of the state. He was, to the end, a family servant, and not the ruler's, or a public servant. This being so, his most important duty was that of unswerving loyalty to his lord, and to cast off this obligation to the family, and in its place to recognize any form of more binding allegiance to the state, was regarded, according to the morality of the age, as tantamount to open rebellion. I have pointed out above (in Chapter I), that at the time of the decline of the city-state system at the close of the Ch'un-ch'iu period, the loyalty-bond between the powerful families and their private retainers became gradually much more strong, even to the point of developing into the servant-lord relationship of feudalism.

Yet Confucius' action in these three episodes detailed in Chapter XVII of the 'Analects', and his readiness in each case to support a retainer in revolt against the lord of the house he served, appears as a complete contradiction of the social morality of the day. Confucius would have vindicated such action by the

154

consideration that provided someone would help to realize the vision of a renaissance of a 'Chou in the East', it mattered not one bit what kind of a man he was: no questions were asked about his character—he was merely utilized as a means to the end, the realization of the vision. Confucius would have admitted, in each of these situations, that he was violating the conventions of the social morality of his day, in casting in his lot with servants in revolt against their lords, but he justified such conduct on the grounds of the plea that it was the only available, and so the unavoidable means to the translation of the vision into fact.

Yet, if it were really possible to refound the Way of Chou in the East—in fact, to re-establish the Royal Court of Chou—it would be essential to transcend the narrow ruler-servant relationship of the various city-states. The loyalty relation binding family retainer and family head, was even of less moment than this, and could be disregarded. Perhaps Confucius' attitude was something on these lines—the family retainer should be a public servant rather than a private hireling, and the public servant should not be such as much as a servant of Chou. Unless Confucius is pictured as adopting a thorough-going attitude of this nature, there remains the problem of explaining away the distress which he would feel at being obliged to clash with the established morality of his times—the supreme loyalty of the retainer to the family he served. Perhaps the compilers of this chapter, or again, the disciples who were responsible for the handing on of these episodes, unable to shake off the trammels of the feudal lord-servant morality which persisted from the latter part of the Ch'un-ch'iu through the Chan-kuo periods, mistook the true intent of Confucius' drastic criticism of feudal morality.

In Lu, the overweening administration of the 'Three Huan', and the Chi family had incurred the indignation of Confucius: in Ch'i, he had seen at first hand the tyranny of the Ts'ui, and the Ch'ing families, and the sight had driven him back to Lu. But such harsh governments were not long-lived; in Ch'i, the Ts'ui and the Ch'ing followed each other to destruction, and in Lu, the 'Three Huan' had seemed more than once to be on the verge of disaster. Again Confucius saw with his own eyes the sudden withering of the extravagance of Yang Hu, and he came to realize the transience of the success of the retainer of the noble family. It was in this connection that he said, 'When the Way prevails in the world, ritual, music, and punitive expeditions proceed from the Emperor. When the Way prevails not, ritual, music and punitive expeditions will proceed from the hands of princes. When such things proceed from the princes, they will be few who do not lose their power within the space of ten generations. When they proceed from the Senior Officers of the prince, they will be few who do not lose their place within five generations. And when the Senior Officers' retainers control the administration of the state, they will be few who do not lose their power within three generations. When the Way prevails in the world, government will not be in the hands of the Senior Officers. When the Way prevails in the world, there is no need for discussion among the people.'

In this section, Confucius is shown as drawing attention to the fact that during the period of the Chou dynasty—and especially in Ch'un-ch'iu times—together with the decay of the Royal Way of Chou, there came a gradual transfer of administrative authority to persons of a lower status—a decline from Emperor to prince, then from prince to senior official, from official to family retainer; and in ratio with this change of the seat of power, the length of the period for which power was retained grew proportionately shorter. These words, again from a section belonging to the 'Later Analects' would be produced sometime during the Chan-kuo (or 'Warring States') period, at the time when the book by the name of the 'Ch'un-ch'iu', (of which Confucius was supposed to have been the compiler, with the state chronicle of Lu as the basis, and with the addition to it of notes of criticism of the times) had become a highly venerated classic for one of the schools of Confucianism which flourished in the state of Ch'i.

Such a coldly objective view of history, together with the achievement of a mental outlook wherewith he could follow the fate of the upstarts, and give a secret shout of joy at their demise, and tell these tales of nemesis and retribution as warnings to his disciples—this would be a state which Confucius could attain only in his later years. The younger Confucius still hoped that influential families like the Chi in Lu and the T'ien in Ch'i, whose authority was not to be easily dislodged, might be overthrown, and the administrative control of the state which they had monopolized might be returned to the hands of the rightful prince: this he believed to be the most pressing need of the age, and it was for its realization that he gave his utmost efforts.

The general principle governing Confucius' policy of political reform was the overthrow of powerful clans such as the Chi family in Lu: he exerted all his powers in an all-out effort to realize this end. Confucius gradually obtained sympathizers with his aims in Lu, and as he attracted able pupils and constituted a school, so he came to be better known. The spread of his fame is shown by the interest in him evinced by Yang Hu; Yang Hu had amassed in his own hands the governmental control of the entire state, had utilized internal disputes within the Chi family in furtherance of his scheme to disturb the regular succession to the headship of the family, and of the other two of the 'Three Huan' families, and finally planned to murder all the family elders. That he should have been keeping a careful eye on Confucius—whose political views were hardly sympathetic—and that he should have attempted to win him over, and to make use of Confucius in the execution of his own schemes of aggrandisement, is by no means unnatural, but an extremely reasonable development. In comparison, the problem of the historicity of the episodes concerning the invitations to Confucius from the retainer of the Chi house, Kung-shan Fu-jao, and the Chao family official Fu Hsi, is now very much more difficult to decide. The clear fact remains, however, that Confucius' views involved the rejection of the retainer's loyalty to his master, and the exertion of a supreme effort on behalf of the ducal house.

This attitude, with its basis in the tenets of Confucius' political philosophy, is the core of the 'Ch'un-ch'iu', the didactic history, which was in all probability completed by the disciples. Perhaps the clearest manifestation of this outlook is to be found in the violent criticism, in the 'Kung-yang Commentary'—one of the three expositions by different schools of the text of the 'Ch'un-ch'iu'— of the practice whereby high offices, such as that of premier, were made hereditary.

5 Failure of the Revolution

Yang Hu, the retainer of the Chi house, had for a period of three years held absolute control of the government of Lu, and his final coup, the attempt to overturn the 'Three Huan', merely caused a severe shock to the people of Lu, who had long suffered at the mercy of the absolutism of the Chi family. From the point of view of the ducal house, the authority of the 'Three Huan', which hitherto had seemed so firmly rooted as to be unassailable, was now clearly revealed as something that could be overthrown, and the hope of a restoration of power to the hands of the rightful prince was to some extent disclosed. From the aspect of the 'Three Huan' themselves, there was felt the need for a thorough investigation into the reason why their authority should crumble so readily.

However, the most important and immediate task was the reconstitution of the order of both government and society, which had been sadly disrupted by the usurping politics of Yang Hu: it was imperative to eradicate the errors of the policies adopted hitherto by the 'Three Huan', and to formulate a new over-all plan of benefit to the entire state. Within the families of the 'Three Huan', there was, regrettably, not a single member gifted with the talents necessary for the introduction of such a new programme. In such circumstances, the image of Confucius would float large in the minds of many—the Confucius whose political knowledge and judgment Yang Hu had tried hard to buy, and whom he had attempted, by every means at his disposal, to make a servant of his family, and whose verbal promise of service, at least, he had at length succeeded in securing.

Confucius' first official position, that of mayor of the town of Chung-tu, can be surmised to have been assumed in the year 501 B.C., just at the time when Yang Hu's grandiose schemes had met with failure after his single defeat, and he had fled the state to Ch'i. At this time, Confucius had just reached the age of fifty. The ancient social conventions of China laid strict emphasis on distinctions made according to age. On reaching the age of forty, a man became a member of a group known as 'Ch'iang'—strong men and true—and only then was he regarded as qualified to assume office, and take a part in the government of his state. At fifty, entering a class known as 'Ai'—the veterans—he was regarded as an elder, and advanced to the administrative rank of 'senior officer', which carried with it the competency to supervise a number of officials junior to him. Confucius had just passed the requisite age limit of fifty years at this time, and the dating to this year of his appointment to the mayoralty of Chung-tu—which would carry with it a position of authority over a number of lesser officials and would be ranked as a post appropriate to a 'senior officer'—harmonizes perfectly with the convention mentioned above. This hypothesis should then be regarded as fairly reliable.

In the following year, Confucius rose to even greater prominence, for he took part, as a member of the retinue of Duke Ting of Lu, in a peace conference with Ch'i. At this conference, the adviser to Duke Ching of Ch'i was the famous minister Yen Tzu, who included a group of aborigines from the east in his party, scheming to apply threats to Lu in the course of the conference and to force the acceptance of unfavourable conditions on her. Confucius saw through the plot, and then and there scolded the aborigines who were to have burst in on the conference, carrying weapons. The story of his parrying of misfortune before it fell, and his being able to bring the conference to a successful end for Lu is told in each of the three commentaries to the 'Ch'un-ch'iu' history.

After this successful conclusion of the peace conference with Ch'i, Confucius' popularity with the people of Lu jumped suddenly. In the following year, 499 B.C., he was appointed to the office of Minister of Crime, the highest judicial function in the state, and simultaneously held some kind of diplomatic post. Over a long period, Lu had associated herself with the Northern League, with Tsin at its head, but in this year, Confucius made a clean break with the League. Actually, one of the most important factors which had enabled the 'Three Huan' to maintain their autocratic control of the government of Lu, lay in the fact that they used to pay bribes to the six influential families of Tsin, and in close alliance with them, were able to dragoon the prince of Lu, with the influence of the League leader to back them. This withdrawal from the Northern League was not actuated by the dictates of Confucius' foreign policy: it was rather part of an attempt to arrest the treachery of the 'Three Huan', who, in league with Tsin, and by allowing her to meddle in and control Lu's internal affairs, hoped to strengthen the position of their own households. Confucius' plan for the overthrow of the 'Three Huan' then started with this re-orientation in foreign policy. Never allowing his attention to be absorbed completely by internal conditions in Lu, but above all working for an improvement in Lu's international position, Confucius was no mere provincial politician with his horizon bounded by the limits of his own state; instead, with his rich international knowledge and experience, he towered far above his contemporaries, a man with the vision of a true statesman.

With the execution of this switch in foreign policy, which denied to the influential families, such as the 'Three Huan', the scope of interfering, with the power of Tsin to support them, in the internal affairs of the state, and with the freeing of Lu from any constraining pressure from without, Confucius embarked on a policy aimed at containing the power of the 'Three Huan' in internal politics also. The influence of the 'Three Huan' depended above all on their private military strength. Of their forces, the part permanently quartered within the walls of the capital was probably not very great; but the base strongholds of each family, placed at vulnerable points in their domains, such as Pi, belonging to the Chi family, Hou of the Shu-sun family, and Ch'eng of the Meng-sun family, were all well fortified, and contained a large garrison of troops and fully-stocked armouries. If the city mansion of the family were to suffer an unexpected attack, a fresh relieving force could be sent at a moment's notice from these bases. In the final analysis, the source of the power of the 'Three Huan' lay in the three strongpoints of Pi, Hou and Ch'eng.

Confucius fully realized that these three forts, the basis of the power of the 'Three Huan', could never be demolished by the coercion of either the prince of Lu, or of the rest of the high officials of the state. The 'Three Huan' must carry out the demolition with their own hands. The Chi family had just witnessed the bitter sight of a dire threat to the existence of their whole house, in the revolt of Yang Hu, the commandant of their fortress Pi, with the military might of the fortress at his back. Confucius made good use of this recent example, and convinced the 'Three Huan' that in order to prevent rebellion by any of their high-handed retainers, their best plan was to dismantle the fortifications of Pi, Hou, and Ch'eng, the bases of the disaffected servants, and to decentralize their forces. Thus the agreement of the 'Three Huan' to his plan was secured.

In 498 B.C., Confucius recommended his most militarily minded disciple, Tzu Lu, to the Chi family, hoping that he would be placed in a position of authority over the rest of the family retainers, and would be given the order by the Chi house to dismantle the defence equipment of their fortress at Pi. The plan went well in these first stages, for after the Chi had dismantled the defence walls of Pi, the Shu-sun house, of their own volition, began the work of destroying the fortifications of their stronghold at Hou. However, there still remained the fort of the Meng-sun family at Ch'eng: they argued that it was a vital strategic base near to the border between Lu and Ch'i, and was in fact something akin to Lu's north gate; destroy this, and an invading Ch'i force could plunder Lu territory without opposition—to say nothing, of course, of its role as the vital headquarters of the Meng-sun house: to demolish it with their own hands was foolhardy in the extreme. They turned a deaf ear to all efforts to win them over, and insisted that it would be for the best not to embark on such work.

As the Meng-sun clan would not demolish their fortifications of their own accord, Confucius prevailed on Duke Ting to lead a force and lay siege to Ch'eng, in an effort to enforce the dismantling by a show of military might. But the defence works of the fort were extremely strong and in the end, the investing force had to retire without success. Thus, after Confucius had deliberately and successfully induced the voluntary demolition of two of the forts of the 'Three Huan', he had come upon an impasse, in the shape of the final remaining fort belonging to the Meng-sun family. But as soon as this delay occurred, the 'Three Huan', who had hitherto been placing complete trust in their agent, must have realized that his objective was in fact the extermination of their respective houses. There is no clear record of the consequence for Confucius of this realization, but, losing their support, he must have fallen from his position of political power.

163

The scheme to overthrow the power of the 'Three Huan' had progressed according to plan until the very final step. Confucius' disappointment at his final failure must have been very bitter. Yet he did not despair at his ill-luck, but, in the following year, he forsook his native state, and set out on a tour of the various kingdoms. And as there is no record that Confucius was ever banished from Lu, it was probably as a free agent and on his own initiative that he left his country.

Confucius had a good understanding of international affairs, and was thus well informed concerning the internal and external policies of the various states of his time. In almost every state, the rightful prince had been rendered ineffective, and there ruled in his place an oligarchy of the noble families. Confucius, it is true, had failed in his attempt to overthrow the powerful families of Lu, but in the other states which he visited, it was his desire to attack the influence of the noble families, retrieve the position and prestige of the prince, and set up his ideal community. It seems that it was with hopes such as these that he set out on his wanderings.

6 The Years of Wandering

It was in the year 497 B.C., that Confucius left Lu, where his scheme had met with failure at the final stage, to travel to the various states of China. His first place of call was the kingdom of Wei, Lu's neighbour to the north-west, and a state which belonged to the culture group of the central plain. After a short stay, he turned south to Sung, Cheng, Ch'en, and Ts'ai, and then, after passing again through Wei, returned finally to Lu in 484 B.C. This long period of thirteen years spent in wandering abroad, was a time of severe trial for Confucius, a time when he was threatened by the greatest crises of his whole life.

164

In his biography of Confucius in the 'Historical Records', Ssu-ma Ch'ien painted a very vivid picture of Confucius in adverse circumstances, and all biographers since his time have followed in the pattern set by him, and have tended to lay rather too much emphasis on the sorry plight of Confucius in the period of his wanderings. The people of the state of Cheng, seeing Confucius roaming about, separated from his disciples, at one of the gates in the walls of their city, are said to have likened his appearance to that of a 'dog from a house of mourning'—that is, roaming about, and seeking for food like a dog uncared for and unfed by a master busy with funeral rites.

Before he went south from Wei, Confucius was for a time minded to stay in Tsin, the head state of the Northern League, but on the way westwards, at a place called K'uang, near to the Yellow River ferrying point, he was attacked by the townspeople who mistook him for someone else, and nearly lost his life. In consequence, he abandoned the plan to enter Tsin, and turned south, with Ch'u, the leader of the southern alliance, as his new objective. But again, before he could reach his destination, he was attacked in Sung by a general named Huan T'ui, and once again, his life was exposed to grave danger. And before he reached Ch'u, in the neighbourhood of the borders between the satellite states Ch'en and Ts'ai, with provisions entirely exhausted, he was obliged to go without food for a whole week.

These three occasions of grave danger to life and limb during the thirteen year period of travel, are recorded in the 'Analects': thus even allowing for a certain degree of exaggerated colouring, it would seem to be true that he did meet with misfortunes of this nature. Yet it would be very wrong to regard Confucius' life in the various states during this period as entirely that of a beggar—that of a 'dog from a house in mourning'.

The success attained by Confucius as a diplomat at the difficult peace congress with Ch'i would most certainly have been talked of among the other states. Again, in spite of the ultimate failure, his name would have been heard of by the learned men of each state, in connection with his restrictive measures against the 'Three Huan', and with his revolutionary policies aimed at the revival of the power of the prince. With his group of disciples, including Yen Hui, Tzu Lu, Tzu Kung, and others, and with a convoy of carriages, he was welcomed with every courtesy by the princes of the countries he visited; they invited him to their courts, and listened attentively to his discourses on government. Duke Ling of the state of Wei especially held Confucius in high regard, and frequently met with him for discussions, and the ruler of the small kingdom of She also availed himself of the opportunity to put questions to him.

Someone once asked the disciple Tzu Kung, 'Whenever your Master comes to a state, he invariably learns about its government. Is it that he asks for this information, or is it given to him?' To this, Tzu Kung replied, 'Our Master is warm and upright, respectful and modest—and it is in virtue of these qualities that he gets his information. The Master's way of asking for information is quite different from that of other men.' That is, in virtue of his modesty, Confucius was naturally given information, and did not himself purposely seek for it. But the fact that he was asked about governmental policy by princes and nobles in every state that he visited, that he did give opinions on the subject, and that he even took part in important affairs of state, appeared as surprising objectives to the men of his age.

During this thirteen year period of travel and residence abroad, Confucius did not by any means live the life of a nameless and unknown scholar, hounded at every turn by poverty and ill-fortune. In fact, it would be no exaggeration to say that the greater part of this period brought for Confucius a spectacular life of endless courteous treatment at the hands of kings, marquises and nobles. But Confucius was by no means content merely to rub shoulders with such personages, and accept their hospitality. His passage from court to court was not simply motivated by the desire to live on the entertainment and hospitality of such people: rather, this was a political crusade, and these rulers and nobles were to be the agents in the realization of his revolutionary political ideals.

The motive which led the various princes to vie among themselves in offering invitations to Confucius, and in wishing to hear his political advice, undoubtedly lay in the curiosity aroused by his very novel attempts to bring about a revolution in Lu. The basic essence of his advice to them would be, as was the case with his reform policy in Lu, first the destruction of the oligarchy of the noble clans, and secondly, the restoration of the authority of the rightful ruler to its ancient and proper place. The various princes would no doubt be very much attracted to such a platform, but the nobles would be strongly and unconditionally opposed to what were, for them, such baleful proposals. For the nobles, Confucius' way of thinking was fraught with extreme danger, and was a dire threat to the very existence of their class.

Confucius' welcome in the courts of the different kingdoms was, in outward appearance, very cordial and warm: yet his political ideal, the destruction of the influential families, was never given a serious hearing.

167

The source of the dangerous situations with which he was threatened in Wei, Sung, and Ch'en, is not at all clearly stated either in the 'Analects' or in any of the biographies. It may well be that, as his revolutionary political ideal—especially the policy aimed at the destruction of the influential families—impinged directly upon the position of these families in each state, they instigated thugs and hirelings to aid them in wiping this dangerous idealist from the face of the earth.

As he went round the courts of the smaller kingdoms, such as Sung, Wei, and Cheng, Confucius expounded his political ideal, but failed to secure any concrete or practical response. So he resolved to have no more dealings with the princes of the smaller states, where court life was strictly circumscribed by convention, and planned to make his way to Tsin, which, as the leader of the northern alliance, held *de facto* control of the central states, or to Ch'u, the opposing leader of the southern league, there to explain the details of his ideal, and to enlist the might of such powerful leaders for the extension of the scope of his proposed reforms to the whole of the Chinese world. However, his plans met with opposition from the smaller states, and, in the end, his ambition was never fulfilled.

When he ran into danger at K'uang, on his way from Wei to Tsin, Confucius exclaimed, 'King Wen died long ago: but is not the cause of culture still alive here? If Heaven had planned to destroy this culture, we who now breathe would not have been enabled to partake of it. Heaven then does not intend to destroy this culture—so what have I to fear at the hands of the men of K'uang?' With these words, Confucius indicated that the Way embodied in the 'Odes', the 'Documents', the Ritual and the Music, all the creations of King Wen, had been transmitted to, and was now being handed on by Confucius himself; and as Heaven had selected him as the vehicle for the transmission of this Way, he was confident that he was not fated to suffer death at the hands of men such as those of the town of K'uang. Confucius here appears not as a lone individual trying to further his ideal, but as one clinging firmly to the conviction that it was in accordance with the dictates of a mandate from Heaven that he was attempting to realize his ideal in the world.

Again, when caught off his guard by the surprise attack of Huan T'ui, a man belonging to a noble family of Sung, Confucius merely remarked, with complete composure, 'If Heaven gave life to the virtue in me, what can this Huan T'ui do to me?' He was the recipient of a mandate from Heaven, and as such, could suffer no harm from the common man. This was the general view of Confucius held by his disciples, who, loving him as their father, and banded together, stuck to him through this long thirteen years of foreign travel.

In spite of his conviction that he had received an injunction from heaven, and that he was born to bring about a reform in the world, Confucius clearly realized that the terms of his mandate would not, in the outcome, be fulfilled in this world. The rational Confucius was fully appreciative of the objective situation; if this command entrusted to him was not capable of realization in his own lifetime, then it must be achieved in the future, by means of the education of his disciples, and the transmission of the ideal, through their agency, to later generations.

The youngest of the disciples who followed Confucius in his journeying, the one whose passion for study was the most ardent, and in whom Confucius placed the greatest reliance and hope was Yen Hui;—but even he was already past the age of thirty. The eldest, Tzu Lu, had reached the age of sixty! Every member of the party, in fact, might be said to have been past his prime. It was not proper to make them old before their time, by asking them to trail after him for ever, with no visible ending to their wanderings. It was considerations such as these which determined Confucius that it would be for the best to return to Lu.

The abandonment of all attempts to realize his ideal in the world cannot have been easy for Confucius, but in the end he brought himself to make the resolve. At the time of his return to Lu after his thirteen years of travel abroad, Duke Ting had long been dead, and his successor, Duke Ai, was in the eleventh year of his reign. This was in 484 B.C., and Confucius was sixty-nine years of age: for the next five years, until his death in 479 B.C., at the age of seventy-four, Confucius bent all his energies to the task of educating his disciples, and setting in order and compiling the old classics, such as the 'Odes' and the 'Documents', which he himself had read and learned. Confucius the statesman was dead: but in these duties, the final activities of Confucius the educator, and Confucius the scholar still continued.

CONCLUSION

THE PHILOSOPHER'S DEATH

Confucius died in 479 B.C. The notice of his death is clearly recorded in the classic of the 'Ch'un-ch'iu', which had as its base the official state chronicle of Lu, the kingdom which Confucius served as an official. The record reads, under the sixteenth year of Duke Ai, 'Summer, a day in the fourth month, Confucius died.' In this particular, then, there is practically no room for doubt. On the other hand, the dates recorded for the birth of the son of Shu-liang Ho, whose status was merely that of an impoverished knight in the service of the head of the Meng clan, seem to be no more than a part of a tradition which grew up much later. Stories of Confucius collecting three thousand disciples are clearly exaggerations: yet, the picture of Confucius revered as the sage of the times, and surrounded by the seventy talented disciples, enamoured of his learning and virtue, is also one which only has reference to his last years. We must try to paint in a little more detail the events of the last years of 'the philosopher'. The account recorded in the chapter called 'T'an Kung' of the Record of Ritual—a work which listed precedents having reference to the ritual of mourning and bereavement, and the discussions of Confucian scholars on such topics—is part of this tradition which should be examined.

Just seven days before his death, Confucius arose early, and, shuffling along with the aid of his staff, strolled outside the gate, and began to recite a poem: 'Mount T'ai will crumble; The bridge will fall; The Sage shall languish'. At the end of the poem, he entered the room, and sat himself down facing the door. Tzu Kung, who, after the death of Yen Hui was the most talented of the remaining disciples, heard of what had happened, and realizing that Confucius' illness was growing more critical, came rushing to him. Confucius met him with the words, 'Why have you been so long in coming? In Hsia times, the coffin was placed at the eastern staircase of the hall; in Yin times, it was placed between the two pillars at the centre of the hall, and under the Chou, the coffin lay by the western staircase. Now I am descended from the Yin people, but one night, I dreamed that I was sat between the two pillars, and that the food offered to the dead was placed before me. Alas! No wise ruler appears. Who will there be in the world to take me for a master? My life will not be long now.' And he took to his bed, and after a week of sickness, he died.

This tradition is explained by Cheng Hsüan, a commentator who lived in Han times, as indicating that the Sage was perfectly aware that he was the recipient of a mandate from Heaven; yet, grieving over the fact that no enlightened prince came forward to employ him, and utterly despairing of the present world, he laid himself down on his bed of sickness and passed on. But are these really acts worthy of the sage of the times, and can these actions and thoughts really be said to be a reflection of the composure of one who knew the mandate of Heaven? This is the first doubt to strike the reader of this passage of the tradition. Soon, Wu Ch'eng, a Yüan dynasty scholar, argued that Confucius' wandering before his house leaning on his staff, his grief at the approach of death, shown in the composition of a song in the course of which he referred to himself as a sage— all this could hardly be understood as the last acts of a sage who transcended the bonds of life and death, and who was unconcernedly content in his destiny. Nor was there any lack of scholars who made similar attacks upon this ridiculous tradition.

Yet such a controversy, with the implication of the subjective and hypothetical picture of the sage transcending all bonds of life and death, has no very sound or proven basis. Completely contrary to such arguments, Confucius was not the transcendent sage, but, as far as lay in his power, the human sage. Far from being able to escape from the restrictions of life and death, he persevered to the end in what he considered was the function ordained for him in the world, and never succeeded in dispelling the awe of death. A refutation of the above interpretation, based on these latter factors is also quite feasible, and is, in fact, much more appropriate to the death of the master.

One of the advocates of the latter view, Ts'ui Shu, contends that after the general modesty of Confucius' words throughout the 'Analects',—where there is not a single context in which Confucius appears as thinking of himself as a sage, or discusses prosperity and evil fortune; he only clarifies what kind of action is demanded by righteousness,—this metaphorical self-comparison to Mount T'ai, to a bridge, and to a sage, and the prediction by means of a dream of the omens portending his death, are not to be considered as a fair representation of the topics or the mode of Confucius' everyday conversation. It would be well worth our while to consider such contentions a little more deeply. At least none will deny that the song, the centre piece of the story, was not Confucius' own composition, and it will probably be agreed, in consequence, that this tradition concerning the predictions made by Confucius about his death, which was constituted around the spurious song as the keystone, gradually took shape among the immediate disciples, or the later scholars of the Confucian school. Although this story may be only one of a series of similar traditions, there must have been some cause for these tales to have arisen among the later disciples, and I now wish to discuss the problem of the historical background in which a tradition of this nature could have taken shape.

The peculiar feature of this story, is the deeply imprinted sense of despair of the world of the time. Disillusion of this nature must have been occasioned, above all, by a fierce annoyance with humanity and society. Yet there is a wide gap between this attitude, and that

173

which appears behind his statement of his resignation to what fate had in store, as he recollected the stages of his life and progress, in his later years—'At fifteen, my heart was set on study; at thirty, I was established; at forty, I had no doubts, and at fifty, I knew Heaven's will; at sixty, my ear was obedient, and at seventy, I could follow the desires of my heart and not transgress the limits of the right.' Nevertheless, in the Confucius of old age, there does seem to have been an undercurrent of a feeling in some ways akin to a sense of disillusion. There would certainly be vague stirrings of the consciousness of loneliness in his academic activities, in spite of his being surrounded by so many devoted disciples. This loneliness is shown at its clearest in Confucius' recollections of his beloved disciple Yen Hui, who had died suddenly and at an early age. The unexpected deaths of both Chang-tzu Po-yü, and Yen Hui (Po-yü was Confucius' eldest son), threw Confucius into the depths of despondency, and it might even be thought that their impact in some measure hastened his death. There is no clear statement of the date of the deaths of Po-yü and Yen Hui, although both appear to have occurred soon after Confucius' return from his long period of travel outside of Lu, a few years, that is, before the death of Confucius himself. Asked by Duke Ai, the prince of Lu, which of the disciples loved learning the most, Confucius replied, 'Yen Hui; he loved learning. He never vented his anger on others, never repeated a fault. Unfortunately, he died young, and now he is gone. I do not know of any who loves learning as he did.' This reply reveals the feelings of reverence which Confucius held for his most learned disciple.

Confucius' confidence in Yen Hui is too well-known to need elaboration here. The only disciple at all comparable to him in talent and learning was Tzu Kung;

and asked by Confucius which of the two, he himself or Yen Hui, excelled the more, Tzu Kung replied, 'How dare I compare myself with Hui? Tell Hui one point, and he would know ten; told one point, I would only know two.' Talented though he was, Tzu Kung was yet several stages inferior to Yen Hui. To this reply Confucius made his own significant comment,—'No. You are not up to his standard. Neither you nor I are as good as he.' Confucius here even places himself on a plane below Yen Hui, and always insisted that it was only Yen Hui who fully understood the ways of thought which he himself embraced, and thoroughly grasped the essence of his teachings.

One day, perhaps after the death of Yen Hui, Confucius groaned as he lamented, 'Nobody knows me.' Tzu Kung, who sat in waiting on him, asked, 'What do you mean when you say that no one knows you?' Tzu Kung perhaps felt that it was somewhat pointless on Confucius' part to complain that nobody knew him, when Tzu Kung himself understood his Master. Again, there was possibly an undercurrent of slight jealousy in that the Master was once again harking back to the memory of Yen Hui. Perhaps Confucius was in fact pining for Yen Hui; at any rate, he completely altered the drift of the conversation at this point, and went on, 'I harbour no feelings of resentment against Heaven; I lay blame at the feet of no man; my study below penetrates on high. Is it Heaven then that knows me?' None knew him, or recognized his abilities, but he was not, on that account, resentful against Heaven, nor did he seek to lay the blame on any man. If a man simply put his soul into study, he would, by a natural process, penetrate to Heaven. Thus, after all, Heaven knew him.

Confucius' comparison of himself with Heaven in this context has a deep significance, a fuller explanation of which demands reference to a statement made by Tzu Kung, of which neither the date nor the context is clear. Tzu Kung declared, 'The Master's writings are a topic about which one can hear; but his discourses about human nature and Heaven's way—these cannot be heard.' The reference to Confucius' writings, according to the commentators, is to be explained in concrete terms as a pointer to the classic texts of the 'Odes' and the 'Documents', which he set his disciples to read, and to the precepts of the ritual and the music which he had them carry out in their actions. Confucius taught his disciples by means of these writings, but, distinct from the classics, and the rules of ritual and ceremonial, there was no means of explaining to them either the nature of mankind, or the laws of Heaven which controlled the world.

The import of the statement of Tzu Kung is, by and large, true to fact. Confucius never thought directly in terms of the problems of either the nature of mankind, or the laws of Heaven. I have provisionally interpreted Heaven's way as 'the laws of Heaven'; the ancient Chinese, however, did not recognize, and put their faith in a single and supreme heavenly spirit, possessed of a divine nature, and controlling all life and matter in the world. According to the views of the commentators of both the Han and Ch'ing dynasties, belief in Heaven's way comprised a faith based in the magic of astrological belief, which followed the courses of the sun and moon, and the other heavenly bodies, and put faith in the efficacy of good and bad fortune derived therefrom, and affecting the natural and the human world. The concept of Heaven was not that of a supreme deity possessed of human personality and will; the image invoked was much more that of a nature spirit, embodied in the movements of the heavenly bodies.

The clarification of the principles of the relation between these movements and the affairs of man, and the attempt to predict the cycle of good and bad fortune in accordance with such pre-indications, was the special art of the sorcerers, the masters of divination in ancient China, for whose arts Confucius had not the slightest support or sympathy.

Confucius, who never made 'wonders, feats of strength, supernatural disorders, or the spirits' a part of his conversation or education, positively rejected any such astrological faiths, and beliefs based on shamanistic sorcery, his attitude being determined principally by the spirit of rationalism of his age. Confucius defined knowledge, in a passage which I have already quoted above, in terms of 'striving for the righteousness of the people, and, while showing due respect for the spirits, keeping them at a safe distance.' He believed, then, that the most essential prerequisite for the acquisition of knowledge lay in giving a wide berth to any faiths which had to do with the prevalent superstitions of his age.

The reason for the rejection of religion in this manner is stated in Confucius' answer to the question from Tzu Lu concerning the celebrations and service which should be offered to the spirits—'You cannot yet serve man adequately; how would you properly render service to the spirits'; and, in reply to the further enquiry about death, 'You do not know anything about life yet; why should you know about death?' Problems such as the unknown nature of life after death in another world were put off by Confucius as unknowable, and his aim was instead to make clear the significance and meaning of our experiences in our life in the present world. Again, in regard to one's actions in life, Confucius said, 'Hear as much as you can, and put aside what strikes you as doubtful, and then be cautious in speaking of what remains;—then there will be few faults in your action. See much, cut out what seems to you to be dangerous, and be cautious in acting on what remains; then your regrets will not be many.' In other words, Confucius here advises the widest and richest possible range of experience, both visual and aural, and the elimination of any doubtful element from the knowledge which comes of that experience. This maxim was offered as a general rule covering all actions in life, but it could well be regarded also as exemplifying Confucius' formula for the formation of a body of knowledge, and his prescription for study methods. Confucius also said, 'Knowledge consists in regarding what one knows as the known, and what one does not know as the unknown'. Any phenomenon which is obscure and not clear to the intellect is excluded as rigorously as possible, and knowledge is regarded as made up only of parts which leave not the slightest room for doubt to the intellect. Anything occult is rejected, the rational only is retained. Yet it could not be argued that, in any strict sense, any concrete example of what Confucius would have understood to be doubtful, would be classified as doubtful to what is meant by reason in the modern sense, nor that what Confucius regarded as the knowable, or the known would be self-evident to reason in the modern sense of the term. Confucius said of himself, 'I transmit, and do not create; I have a love of, and faith in, the past.' The way of the ancients, anything traditional that is, is self-evident, and is of value; in this attitude, Confucius clearly retains a strong tendency to traditionalism. On the other hand, he argued that, 'A son who for three years does not alter from the way of his father may be called filial.' This implies the rider that after the lapse of the three year limit, an improvisation on the con-

178

ventional behaviour bequeathed by the father is permissible. It seems then that innovations in tradition and convention are not prohibited unconditionally; rather, Confucius realized the need for the renovation and rationalization of tradition, and he went as far as to add his own refinements, provided, of course, that the latter did not conflict with his feelings of fondness for the original form.

Although Confucius' rationalism demanded the rejection of anything of the mystic, he was not thereby committed to a dogmatic disbelief in religious matters in general. When he said, 'Sacrifice to a spirit other than of one's own kin, is mere flattery,'—disapproving, that is, of any celebration in honour of a spirit other than that of an ancestor of one's own family,—he did not intend his words to be construed as an impassable barrier to the preservation intact of the traditional worship and celebrations in honour of the ancestral deities of the clan and of the family; rather was he attempting here to prevent the infiltration of the new religion of the sorcery masters, and to preserve the original purity of the old feudal ritual celebrations. Confucius' attitude, as shown in his words in the 'Analects', demanded the refusal to regard problems of a religious nature as something worthy of consideration in the matter of learning. Such problems were best left alone.

Until his return to Lu, and his concentration on the duty of education in the last years of his life, Confucius devoted all his powers as a statesman to the overthrow of the influential families, and the reinforcement of the authority of the prince. Up to this point, his whole effort was put forth for the realization in his time, and in his world, of his political ideal and as such, his activities were bound up with the present. However, after he had lost hope in his political ambitions, and had ceased to think in terms of the realization of his ideal in the present world, he turned educator, and began teaching his disciples about his aims and ideals, or compiling books which depicted the ideals, and were to be passed on to future generations. Once he had begun in this way to look forward and provide for the realization of the ideal by later generations, the future must have come to take on a greater significance for him than the present.

For Confucius the active statesman, such matters of the far-distant future were no doubt nothing of a problem. But for Confucius the educator-scholar, the dim future subsequent to his own death did become a matter of concern. Of course it would be rash to try to maintain that the future was completely blotted from view in the earlier half of Confucius' life; it did, however, turn into a much more urgent question for him in his later years. He gradually came to take into account the hopes and possibilities of the future; hitherto, mysticism, and any art which attempted to predict future events, he had never concerned himself with; but of late, they turned into a serious problem for him. But would his disciples fully realize the seriousness of the problem even if he gave them a full explanation of the change which had come about in his attitude? Talk of the future was, in the parlance of the times, talk of 'Heaven's will', and as Tzu Kung and his fellow disciples had said, Confucius until then had hardly ever made reference to 'Heaven's will'. Hence even if Confucius were to broach this topic with his disciples, it was likely that not one of them would regard it in any way as a problem—and he had never adopted the technique of being the first to open up a subject; the first question on it must come from the disciples. Once he was on the point of telling them, but held his tongue, and said simply, 'I wish that I had nothing to say.' He meant that though indeed there was something that he did wish to say, it was in fact a thing that could not be said.

Tzu Kung took up the words and objected, 'But if our Master say nothing, what shall we, the disciples, have to hand on to others?' Confucius rejoined, 'But, surely, does Heaven speak? The four seasons come round in their turn, every living thing comes to birth— yet does Heaven have anything to say?' Confucius wanted to speak about matters which concerned Heaven, but 'Heaven's way' was revealed naturally in the progress of the four seasons, and in the creation of the living beings of the universe. And to speak on such topics was, in fact, to expound mysticism; hence, Confucius avoided the subject. This episode reveals to some extent the dilemma in which Confucius' thinking in his later years placed him.

Although Confucius planned to discuss 'Heaven's will' with his disciples, in the end he did not mention the topic even to the most talented of them, such as Tzu Kung. Then, they began to suspect that their Master had some problem which he would not reveal to them, and at this point, Confucius was forced to declare to them, 'Do you think that there is something which I am hiding from you? I hide nothing from you.' It is perhaps not idle to suppose that it was the problem of 'Heaven's will' that was here being concealed from the disciples.

As text-books for the disciples, Confucius invariably used the 'Odes' and the 'Documents', which are the only two of the classics ever to be quoted by him in the 'Analects'. Neither of them was a systematic work, and neither gave any cohesive exposition of the abstract problem of 'Heaven's will'. Apart from these two, the classics of Confucianism also included the 'Book of Changes', and the 'Ch'un-ch'iu', neither of which is referred to or quoted by Confucius in any context in the 'Analects'. The usual inference from this fact is that neither was a compilation which came from Confucius' own hand, but that they are the work of his disciples, or of the disciples in the second generation. Later, the 'Book of Changes' was used as a reference work by the devotees of the craft of sorcery, who predicted the future by divination from the indications gained from the tortoise shell or from the milfoil. The 'Ch'un-ch'iu' was thought to be from the hand of Confucius, with the official state chronicle of Lu as the basis, to which were added comments the purpose of which was to discipline the evil, and to praise the good; it also contained allusions to the ideal political system, the realization of which was here regarded as an event of the future. The element common to these two works is the reference each has to the future; both are works in which 'Heaven's will' has become a point at issue. It may not be too fanciful to suppose that Confucius, for whom 'Heaven's will' had become an issue in his late years, made secret use of these works as aids, and kept the disciples to the end ignorant of this. Then some considerable time after Confucius' death, the works were re-discovered, and selected for use as reference works within the school.

Confucius could find no approval for the world of his times in which influences for evil the like of the 'Three Huan' flourished, for his ideal demanded their overthrow, together with that of every influential family, and the reinstatement in authority of the rightful ruler. He saw that he could not realize his aims in his own lifetime, and had to be content to commit their fulfilment to the future. Now the 'Ch'un-ch'iu', most of all of the classics, did entrust the realization of the ideal to the future; it contains violent criticism of the despotism of influential families, and their usurpation, as hereditary privileges, of important offices of state. Beneath the words of the 'Ch-un-ch'iu', there is a persistent undercurrent of the unattained aims—the destruction of the autocracy of the influential families.

The shift in Confucius' way of thinking in his late years went unnoticed by even the perceptive disciples, such as Tzu Kung; much less could there have been any comprehension of it on the part of the young Tzu Chang, Tzu Yu, Tzu Hsia, and the rest, who only became members of the school during Confucius' last years. With none to understand him, Confucius left the world with feelings of excessive loneliness.

However, his way of thought gradually spread in the world, after the appearance of the 'Ch'un-ch'iu'—to which he was reputed to have made his own additions. His political ideal, the destruction of the noble government of the city-states, and the strengthening of the power of the princes, was adapted to the bureaucratic system of the administration of the 'Seven States' which came to the fore in the Chan-kuo period, and it became the basis on which was founded the theory of the centralized bureaucracy of the Ch'in and Han Empires. Confucius' teachings were adopted as the official doctrine of the Han Empire; three hundred and fifty years in the future, his ideal had gained complete victory.

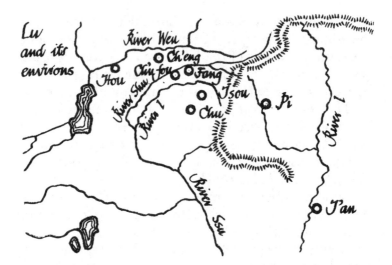

Lu
and its
environs

River Wen
Ch'eng
Ch'u-fou
Hou
River Shu
Fang
Tsou
River I
Chu
Pi
River I
River Ssu
T'an

China in the
Ch'un-ch'iu
period

Yen
Ch'i
Lin-tse
Tsin
Wei
Ts'ao
Chu-fou
Ch'in
Cheng
Sung
Chou
Hsü
Ch'en
Yung
Tsung-Chou
Ts'ai
Wu
Ch'u
Yüeh

CHRONOLOGICAL TABLE

DATE BY WESTERN CONNOTATION	CHOU KING DATE	LU DUKE DATE	EVENT
End of second millenium B.C.			*Fall of the Yin Empire, replaced by Chou.*
			Start of 'Western Chou' period.
Late second millenium B.C.			*Po Ch'in, son of Duke of Chou, enfeoffed in Ch'ü-fou, and founding of state of Lu.*
770 B.C.			*Chou royal seat transferred east from Hsi-an, in Shensi province, to Loyang in Ho-nan province.*
			Start of 'Eastern Chou' period.
722 B.C.	P'ing 49	Yin 1	*Start of the 'Ch'un-ch'iu' period.*
710 B.C.	Huan 10	Huan 2	*K'ung Fu-chia, supposed ancestor of Confucius, murdered in riots in state of Sung.*
685 B.C. to	Chuang 12	Chuang 9	⎱ *Hegemony of Ch'i, under the rule*
664 B.C.	Hsiang 8	Hsi 16	⎰ *of Duke Huan.*
636 B.C. to	Hsiang 16	Hsi 24	⎱ *Hegemony of Tsin, under the rule*
628 B.C.	Hsiang 24	Hsi 32	⎰ *of Duke Wen.*
563 B.C.	Ling 9	Hsiang 10	*Confucius' father, Shu-liang Ho, distinguished conduct at the battle of Pi-yang.*
556 B.C.	Ling 16	Hsiang 17	*Shu-liang Ho penetrates the lines of the investing Ch'i forces at Fang, and makes contact with the relieving Lu army.*
554 B.C.	Ling 18	Hsiang 19	*Tzu Ch'an made a minister of Cheng.*
552 B.C.	Ling 20	Hsiang 21	*Birth of Confucius.*
546 B.C.	Ling 26	Hsiang 27	*Peace congress at Sung between Northern and Southern Leagues, lead by Tsin and Ch'u respectively.*
543 B.C.	Ching 2	Hsiang 30	*Tzu Ch'an becomes premier of Cheng.*
538 B.C.	Ching 7	Chao 4	*Confucius fifteen years of age: becomes a student.*
537 B.C.	Ching 8	Chao 5	*The 'Three Huan' divide the military forces of Lu into three divisions, and control them.*
536 B.C.	Ching 9	Chao 6	*Tzu Ch'an of Cheng has codified law inscribed on bronze vessels.*

DATE BY WESTERN CONNOTATION	CHOU KING DATE	LU DUKE DATE	EVENT
525 B.C.	Ching 20	Chao 17	Confucius 28. Visit to Lu court of Viscount of T'an, and questioned about ancient administrative regulations.
522 B.C.	Ching 23	Chao 20	Death of Tzu Ch'an of Cheng.
517 B.C.	Ching 3	Chao 25	The 'Three Huan' attack Duke Chao of Lu, and force him to flee to Ch'i. Start of period of interregnum in Lu. Confucius, in 36th year, follows Duke Chao to Ch'i.
513 B.C.	Ching 7	Chao 29	State of Tsin has codified law inscribed on bronzes.
510 B.C.	Ching 10	Chao 32	Death outside his kingdom of Duke Chao of Lu. Confucius, in 43rd year, returns to Lu at about this period.
509 B.C.	Ching 11	Ting 1	End of interregnum period in Lu, with accession of Duke Ting.
505 B.C.	Ching 15	Ting 5	Yang Hu of Lu forces oath from his lord, head of the Chi house. Start of tyranny of Yang Hu. Confucius in 48th year. Attempts of Yang Hu to persuade Confucius to join his regime at this period.
502 B.C.	Ching 18	Ting 8	'Three Huan' attack and expel Yang Hu; end of his period of tyranny. Confucius in 51st year. Summons from Kung-shan Fu-jao, steward of Chi house, at this time.
501 B.C.	Ching 19	Ting 9	Flight of Yang Hu to Ch'i. Confucius 52. First takes office in Lu at this period.
500 B.C.	Ching 20	Ting 10	Conference between Ch'i and Lu. Yen Tzu of Ch'i dies. Confucius attends the peace conference as a diplomatic official; gains success.
498 B.C.	Ching 22	Ting 12	Attempt by Duke Ting, following policy of Confucius, to demolish the strongpoints held by the 'Three Huan'. Confucius, in 55th year, fails in attempt to destroy influence of 'Three Huan'.
497 B.C.	Ching 23	Ting 13	Confucius, in 56th year, leaves Lu to travel; goes first to Wei.
494 B.C.	Ching 26	Ai 1	Accession of Duke Ai. Confucius, aged 59, at about this time, leaves Wei and goes to Ch'en.

186

DATE BY WESTERN CONNOTA- TION	CHOU KING DATE	LU DUKE DATE	EVENT
484 B.C.	Ching 36	Ai 11	*Confucius, in 69th year, returns to Lu.*
482 B.C.	Ching 38	Ai 13	*Conference of leagues of Tsin and Wu at Huang-ch'ih.*
481 B.C.	Ching 39	Ai 14	*Duke Ai takes a unicorn while hunting. This interpreted as portent indicating the end of the 'Ch'un-ch'iu' period.*
479 B.C.	Ching 41	Ai 16	*Confucius' death, in 74th year.*

INDEX

THE END

A CATALOG OF SELECTED
DOVER BOOKS
IN ALL FIELDS OF INTEREST

A CATALOG OF SELECTED DOVER
BOOKS IN ALL FIELDS OF INTEREST

CONCERNING THE SPIRITUAL IN ART, Wassily Kandinsky. Pioneering work by father of abstract art. Thoughts on color theory, nature of art. Analysis of earlier masters. 12 illustrations. 80pp. of text. 5⅜ x 8½. 23411-8

ANIMALS: 1,419 Copyright-Free Illustrations of Mammals, Birds, Fish, Insects, etc., Jim Harter (ed.). Clear wood engravings present, in extremely lifelike poses, over 1,000 species of animals. One of the most extensive pictorial sourcebooks of its kind. Captions. Index. 284pp. 9 x 12. 23766-4

CELTIC ART: The Methods of Construction, George Bain. Simple geometric techniques for making Celtic interlacements, spirals, Kells-type initials, animals, humans, etc. Over 500 illustrations. 160pp. 9 x 12. (Available in U.S. only.) 22923-8

AN ATLAS OF ANATOMY FOR ARTISTS, Fritz Schider. Most thorough reference work on art anatomy in the world. Hundreds of illustrations, including selections from works by Vesalius, Leonardo, Goya, Ingres, Michelangelo, others. 593 illustrations. 192pp. 7⅛ x 10¼. 20241-0

CELTIC HAND STROKE-BY-STROKE (Irish Half-Uncial from "The Book of Kells"): An Arthur Baker Calligraphy Manual, Arthur Baker. Complete guide to creating each letter of the alphabet in distinctive Celtic manner. Covers hand position, strokes, pens, inks, paper, more. Illustrated. 48pp. 8¼ x 11. 24336-2

EASY ORIGAMI, John Montroll. Charming collection of 32 projects (hat, cup, pelican, piano, swan, many more) specially designed for the novice origami hobbyist. Clearly illustrated easy-to-follow instructions insure that even beginning papercrafters will achieve successful results. 48pp. 8¼ x 11. 27298-2

THE COMPLETE BOOK OF BIRDHOUSE CONSTRUCTION FOR WOOD-WORKERS, Scott D. Campbell. Detailed instructions, illustrations, tables. Also data on bird habitat and instinct patterns. Bibliography. 3 tables. 63 illustrations in 15 figures. 48pp. 5¼ x 8½. 24407-5

BLOOMINGDALE'S ILLUSTRATED 1886 CATALOG: Fashions, Dry Goods and Housewares, Bloomingdale Brothers. Famed merchants' extremely rare catalog depicting about 1,700 products: clothing, housewares, firearms, dry goods, jewelry, more. Invaluable for dating, identifying vintage items. Also, copyright-free graphics for artists, designers. Co-published with Henry Ford Museum & Greenfield Village. 160pp. 8¼ x 11. 25780-0

HISTORIC COSTUME IN PICTURES, Braun & Schneider. Over 1,450 costumed figures in clearly detailed engravings–from dawn of civilization to end of 19th century. Captions. Many folk costumes. 256pp. 8⅜ x 11¾. 23150-X

STICKLEY CRAFTSMAN FURNITURE CATALOGS, Gustav Stickley and L. & J. G. Stickley. Beautiful, functional furniture in two authentic catalogs from 1910. 594 illustrations, including 277 photos, show settles, rockers, armchairs, reclining chairs, bookcases, desks, tables. 183pp. 6½ x 9¼.   23838-5

AMERICAN LOCOMOTIVES IN HISTORIC PHOTOGRAPHS: 1858 to 1949, Ron Ziel (ed.). A rare collection of 126 meticulously detailed official photographs, called "builder portraits," of American locomotives that majestically chronicle the rise of steam locomotive power in America. Introduction. Detailed captions. xi+ 129pp. 9 x 12.   27393-8

AMERICA'S LIGHTHOUSES: An Illustrated History, Francis Ross Holland, Jr. Delightfully written, profusely illustrated fact-filled survey of over 200 American lighthouses since 1716. History, anecdotes, technological advances, more. 240pp. 8 x 10¾.
25576-X

TOWARDS A NEW ARCHITECTURE, Le Corbusier. Pioneering manifesto by founder of "International School." Technical and aesthetic theories, views of industry, economics, relation of form to function, "mass-production split" and much more. Profusely illustrated. 320pp. 6⅛ x 9¼. (Available in U.S. only.)   25023-7

HOW THE OTHER HALF LIVES, Jacob Riis. Famous journalistic record, exposing poverty and degradation of New York slums around 1900, by major social reformer. 100 striking and influential photographs. 233pp. 10 x 7⅞.   22012-5

FRUIT KEY AND TWIG KEY TO TREES AND SHRUBS, William M. Harlow. One of the handiest and most widely used identification aids. Fruit key covers 120 deciduous and evergreen species; twig key 160 deciduous species. Easily used. Over 300 photographs. 126pp. 5⅜ x 8½.   20511-8

COMMON BIRD SONGS, Dr. Donald J. Borror. Songs of 60 most common U.S. birds: robins, sparrows, cardinals, bluejays, finches, more–arranged in order of increasing complexity. Up to 9 variations of songs of each species.
Cassette and manual 99911-4

ORCHIDS AS HOUSE PLANTS, Rebecca Tyson Northen. Grow cattleyas and many other kinds of orchids–in a window, in a case, or under artificial light. 63 illustrations. 148pp. 5⅜ x 8½.   23261-1

MONSTER MAZES, Dave Phillips. Masterful mazes at four levels of difficulty. Avoid deadly perils and evil creatures to find magical treasures. Solutions for all 32 exciting illustrated puzzles. 48pp. 8¼ x 11.   26005-4

MOZART'S DON GIOVANNI (DOVER OPERA LIBRETTO SERIES), Wolfgang Amadeus Mozart. Introduced and translated by Ellen H. Bleiler. Standard Italian libretto, with complete English translation. Convenient and thoroughly portable–an ideal companion for reading along with a recording or the performance itself. Introduction. List of characters. Plot summary. 121pp. 5¼ x 8½.   24944-1

TECHNICAL MANUAL AND DICTIONARY OF CLASSICAL BALLET, Gail Grant. Defines, explains, comments on steps, movements, poses and concepts. 15-page pictorial section. Basic book for student, viewer. 127pp. 5⅜ x 8½.   21843-0

THE CLARINET AND CLARINET PLAYING, David Pino. Lively, comprehensive work features suggestions about technique, musicianship, and musical interpretation, as well as guidelines for teaching, making your own reeds, and preparing for public performance. Includes an intriguing look at clarinet history. "A godsend," *The Clarinet*, Journal of the International Clarinet Society. Appendixes. 7 illus. 320pp. 5⅜ x 8½. 40270-3

HOLLYWOOD GLAMOR PORTRAITS, John Kobal (ed.). 145 photos from 1926-49. Harlow, Gable, Bogart, Bacall; 94 stars in all. Full background on photographers, technical aspects. 160pp. 8⅜ x 11¼. 23352-9

THE ANNOTATED CASEY AT THE BAT: A Collection of Ballads about the Mighty Casey/Third, Revised Edition, Martin Gardner (ed.). Amusing sequels and parodies of one of America's best-loved poems: Casey's Revenge, Why Casey Whiffed, Casey's Sister at the Bat, others. 256pp. 5⅜ x 8½. 28598-7

THE RAVEN AND OTHER FAVORITE POEMS, Edgar Allan Poe. Over 40 of the author's most memorable poems: "The Bells," "Ulalume," "Israfel," "To Helen," "The Conqueror Worm," "Eldorado," "Annabel Lee," many more. Alphabetic lists of titles and first lines. 64pp. 5$\frac{3}{16}$ x 8¼. 26685-0

PERSONAL MEMOIRS OF U. S. GRANT, Ulysses Simpson Grant. Intelligent, deeply moving firsthand account of Civil War campaigns, considered by many the finest military memoirs ever written. Includes letters, historic photographs, maps and more. 528pp. 6⅛ x 9¼. 28587-1

ANCIENT EGYPTIAN MATERIALS AND INDUSTRIES, A. Lucas and J. Harris. Fascinating, comprehensive, thoroughly documented text describes this ancient civilization's vast resources and the processes that incorporated them in daily life, including the use of animal products, building materials, cosmetics, perfumes and incense, fibers, glazed ware, glass and its manufacture, materials used in the mummification process, and much more. 544pp. 6⅛ x 9¼. (Available in U.S. only.) 40446-3

RUSSIAN STORIES/RUSSKIE RASSKAZY: A Dual-Language Book, edited by Gleb Struve. Twelve tales by such masters as Chekhov, Tolstoy, Dostoevsky, Pushkin, others. Excellent word-for-word English translations on facing pages, plus teaching and study aids, Russian/English vocabulary, biographical/critical introductions, more. 416pp. 5⅜ x 8½. 26244-8

PHILADELPHIA THEN AND NOW: 60 Sites Photographed in the Past and Present, Kenneth Finkel and Susan Oyama. Rare photographs of City Hall, Logan Square, Independence Hall, Betsy Ross House, other landmarks juxtaposed with contemporary views. Captures changing face of historic city. Introduction. Captions. 128pp. 8¼ x 11. 25790-8

AIA ARCHITECTURAL GUIDE TO NASSAU AND SUFFOLK COUNTIES, LONG ISLAND, The American Institute of Architects, Long Island Chapter, and the Society for the Preservation of Long Island Antiquities. Comprehensive, well-researched and generously illustrated volume brings to life over three centuries of Long Island's great architectural heritage. More than 240 photographs with authoritative, extensively detailed captions. 176pp. 8¼ x 11. 26946-9

NORTH AMERICAN INDIAN LIFE: Customs and Traditions of 23 Tribes, Elsie Clews Parsons (ed.). 27 fictionalized essays by noted anthropologists examine religion, customs, government, additional facets of life among the Winnebago, Crow, Zuni, Eskimo, other tribes. 480pp. 6⅛ x 9¼. 27377-6

FRANK LLOYD WRIGHT'S DANA HOUSE, Donald Hoffmann. Pictorial essay of residential masterpiece with over 160 interior and exterior photos, plans, elevations, sketches and studies. 128pp. 9¼ x 10¾. 29120-0

THE MALE AND FEMALE FIGURE IN MOTION: 60 Classic Photographic Sequences, Eadweard Muybridge. 60 true-action photographs of men and women walking, running, climbing, bending, turning, etc., reproduced from rare 19th-century masterpiece. vi + 121pp. 9 x 12. 24745-7

1001 QUESTIONS ANSWERED ABOUT THE SEASHORE, N. J. Berrill and Jacquelyn Berrill. Queries answered about dolphins, sea snails, sponges, starfish, fishes, shore birds, many others. Covers appearance, breeding, growth, feeding, much more. 305pp. 5¼ x 8¼. 23366-9

ATTRACTING BIRDS TO YOUR YARD, William J. Weber. Easy-to-follow guide offers advice on how to attract the greatest diversity of birds: birdhouses, feeders, water and waterers, much more. 96pp. 5³⁄₁₆ x 8¼. 28927-3

MEDICINAL AND OTHER USES OF NORTH AMERICAN PLANTS: A Historical Survey with Special Reference to the Eastern Indian Tribes, Charlotte Erichsen-Brown. Chronological historical citations document 500 years of usage of plants, trees, shrubs native to eastern Canada, northeastern U.S. Also complete identifying information. 343 illustrations. 544pp. 6½ x 9¼. 25951-X

STORYBOOK MAZES, Dave Phillips. 23 stories and mazes on two-page spreads: Wizard of Oz, Treasure Island, Robin Hood, etc. Solutions. 64pp. 8¼ x 11. 23628-5

AMERICAN NEGRO SONGS: 230 Folk Songs and Spirituals, Religious and Secular, John W. Work. This authoritative study traces the African influences of songs sung and played by black Americans at work, in church, and as entertainment. The author discusses the lyric significance of such songs as "Swing Low, Sweet Chariot," "John Henry," and others and offers the words and music for 230 songs. Bibliography. Index of Song Titles. 272pp. 6½ x 9¼. 40271-1

MOVIE-STAR PORTRAITS OF THE FORTIES, John Kobal (ed.). 163 glamor, studio photos of 106 stars of the 1940s: Rita Hayworth, Ava Gardner, Marlon Brando, Clark Gable, many more. 176pp. 8⅜ x 11¼. 23546-7

BENCHLEY LOST AND FOUND, Robert Benchley. Finest humor from early 30s, about pet peeves, child psychologists, post office and others. Mostly unavailable elsewhere. 73 illustrations by Peter Arno and others. 183pp. 5⅜ x 8½. 22410-4

YEKL and THE IMPORTED BRIDEGROOM AND OTHER STORIES OF YIDDISH NEW YORK, Abraham Cahan. Film Hester Street based on *Yekl* (1896). Novel, other stories among first about Jewish immigrants on N.Y.'s East Side. 240pp. 5⅜ x 8½. 22427-9

SELECTED POEMS, Walt Whitman. Generous sampling from *Leaves of Grass*. Twenty-four poems include "I Hear America Singing," "Song of the Open Road," "I Sing the Body Electric," "When Lilacs Last in the Dooryard Bloom'd," "O Captain! My Captain!"–all reprinted from an authoritative edition. Lists of titles and first lines. 128pp. 5³⁄₁₆ x 8¼. 26878-0

THE BEST TALES OF HOFFMANN, E. T. A. Hoffmann. 10 of Hoffmann's most important stories: "Nutcracker and the King of Mice," "The Golden Flowerpot," etc. 458pp. 5⅜ x 8½. 21793-0

FROM FETISH TO GOD IN ANCIENT EGYPT, E. A. Wallis Budge. Rich detailed survey of Egyptian conception of "God" and gods, magic, cult of animals, Osiris, more. Also, superb English translations of hymns and legends. 240 illustrations. 545pp. 5⅜ x 8½. 25803-3

FRENCH STORIES/CONTES FRANÇAIS: A Dual-Language Book, Wallace Fowlie. Ten stories by French masters, Voltaire to Camus: "Micromegas" by Voltaire; "The Atheist's Mass" by Balzac; "Minuet" by de Maupassant; "The Guest" by Camus, six more. Excellent English translations on facing pages. Also French-English vocabulary list, exercises, more. 352pp. 5⅜ x 8½. 26443-2

CHICAGO AT THE TURN OF THE CENTURY IN PHOTOGRAPHS: 122 Historic Views from the Collections of the Chicago Historical Society, Larry A. Viskochil. Rare large-format prints offer detailed views of City Hall, State Street, the Loop, Hull House, Union Station, many other landmarks, circa 1904-1913. Introduction. Captions. Maps. 144pp. 9⅜ x 12¼. 24656-6

OLD BROOKLYN IN EARLY PHOTOGRAPHS, 1865-1929, William Lee Younger. Luna Park, Gravesend race track, construction of Grand Army Plaza, moving of Hotel Brighton, etc. 157 previously unpublished photographs. 165pp. 8⅞ x 11¾. 23587-4

THE MYTHS OF THE NORTH AMERICAN INDIANS, Lewis Spence. Rich anthology of the myths and legends of the Algonquins, Iroquois, Pawnees and Sioux, prefaced by an extensive historical and ethnological commentary. 36 illustrations. 480pp. 5⅜ x 8½. 25967-6

AN ENCYCLOPEDIA OF BATTLES: Accounts of Over 1,560 Battles from 1479 B.C. to the Present, David Eggenberger. Essential details of every major battle in recorded history from the first battle of Megiddo in 1479 B.C. to Grenada in 1984. List of Battle Maps. New Appendix covering the years 1967-1984. Index. 99 illustrations. 544pp. 6½ x 9¼. 24913-1

SAILING ALONE AROUND THE WORLD, Captain Joshua Slocum. First man to sail around the world, alone, in small boat. One of great feats of seamanship told in delightful manner. 67 illustrations. 294pp. 5⅜ x 8½. 20326-3

ANARCHISM AND OTHER ESSAYS, Emma Goldman. Powerful, penetrating, prophetic essays on direct action, role of minorities, prison reform, puritan hypocrisy, violence, etc. 271pp. 5⅜ x 8½. 22484-8

MYTHS OF THE HINDUS AND BUDDHISTS, Ananda K. Coomaraswamy and Sister Nivedita. Great stories of the epics; deeds of Krishna, Shiva, taken from puranas, Vedas, folk tales; etc. 32 illustrations. 400pp. 5⅜ x 8½. 21759-0

THE TRAUMA OF BIRTH, Otto Rank. Rank's controversial thesis that anxiety neurosis is caused by profound psychological trauma which occurs at birth. 256pp. 5⅜ x 8½. 27974-X

A THEOLOGICO-POLITICAL TREATISE, Benedict Spinoza. Also contains unfinished Political Treatise. Great classic on religious liberty, theory of government on common consent. R. Elwes translation. Total of 421pp. 5⅜ x 8½. 20249-6

CATALOG OF DOVER BOOKS

MY BONDAGE AND MY FREEDOM, Frederick Douglass. Born a slave, Douglass became outspoken force in antislavery movement. The best of Douglass' autobiographies. Graphic description of slave life. 464pp. 5⅜ x 8½.   22457-0

FOLLOWING THE EQUATOR: A Journey Around the World, Mark Twain. Fascinating humorous account of 1897 voyage to Hawaii, Australia, India, New Zealand, etc. Ironic, bemused reports on peoples, customs, climate, flora and fauna, politics, much more. 197 illustrations. 720pp. 5⅜ x 8½.   26113-1

THE PEOPLE CALLED SHAKERS, Edward D. Andrews. Definitive study of Shakers: origins, beliefs, practices, dances, social organization, furniture and crafts, etc. 33 illustrations. 351pp. 5⅜ x 8½.   21081-2

THE MYTHS OF GREECE AND ROME, H. A. Guerber. A classic of mythology, generously illustrated, long prized for its simple, graphic, accurate retelling of the principal myths of Greece and Rome, and for its commentary on their origins and significance. With 64 illustrations by Michelangelo, Raphael, Titian, Rubens, Canova, Bernini and others. 480pp. 5⅜ x 8½.   27584-1

PSYCHOLOGY OF MUSIC, Carl E. Seashore. Classic work discusses music as a medium from psychological viewpoint. Clear treatment of physical acoustics, auditory apparatus, sound perception, development of musical skills, nature of musical feeling, host of other topics. 88 figures. 408pp. 5⅜ x 8½.   21851-1

THE PHILOSOPHY OF HISTORY, Georg W. Hegel. Great classic of Western thought develops concept that history is not chance but rational process, the evolution of freedom. 457pp. 5⅜ x 8½.   20112-0

THE BOOK OF TEA, Kakuzo Okakura. Minor classic of the Orient: entertaining, charming explanation, interpretation of traditional Japanese culture in terms of tea ceremony. 94pp. 5⅜ x 8½.   20070-1

LIFE IN ANCIENT EGYPT, Adolf Erman. Fullest, most thorough, detailed older account with much not in more recent books, domestic life, religion, magic, medicine, commerce, much more. Many illustrations reproduce tomb paintings, carvings, hieroglyphs, etc. 597pp. 5⅜ x 8½.   22632-8

SUNDIALS, Their Theory and Construction, Albert Waugh. Far and away the best, most thorough coverage of ideas, mathematics concerned, types, construction, adjusting anywhere. Simple, nontechnical treatment allows even children to build several of these dials. Over 100 illustrations. 230pp. 5⅜ x 8½.   22947-5

THEORETICAL HYDRODYNAMICS, L. M. Milne-Thomson. Classic exposition of the mathematical theory of fluid motion, applicable to both hydrodynamics and aerodynamics. Over 600 exercises. 768pp. 6⅛ x 9¼.   68970-0

SONGS OF EXPERIENCE: Facsimile Reproduction with 26 Plates in Full Color, William Blake. 26 full-color plates from a rare 1826 edition. Includes "The Tyger," "London," "Holy Thursday," and other poems. Printed text of poems. 48pp. 5¼ x 7.
                    24636-1

OLD-TIME VIGNETTES IN FULL COLOR, Carol Belanger Grafton (ed.). Over 390 charming, often sentimental illustrations, selected from archives of Victorian graphics—pretty women posing, children playing, food, flowers, kittens and puppies, smiling cherubs, birds and butterflies, much more. All copyright-free. 48pp. 9¼ x 12¼.
                    27269-9

PERSPECTIVE FOR ARTISTS, Rex Vicat Cole. Depth, perspective of sky and sea, shadows, much more, not usually covered. 391 diagrams, 81 reproductions of drawings and paintings. 279pp. 5⅜ x 8½. 22487-2

DRAWING THE LIVING FIGURE, Joseph Sheppard. Innovative approach to artistic anatomy focuses on specifics of surface anatomy, rather than muscles and bones. Over 170 drawings of live models in front, back and side views, and in widely varying poses. Accompanying diagrams. 177 illustrations. Introduction. Index. 144pp. 8⅜ x11¼. 26723-7

GOTHIC AND OLD ENGLISH ALPHABETS: 100 Complete Fonts, Dan X. Solo. Add power, elegance to posters, signs, other graphics with 100 stunning copyright-free alphabets: Blackstone, Dolbey, Germania, 97 more–including many lower-case, numerals, punctuation marks. 104pp. 8⅛ x 11. 24695-7

HOW TO DO BEADWORK, Mary White. Fundamental book on craft from simple projects to five-bead chains and woven works. 106 illustrations. 142pp. 5⅜ x 8. 20697-1

THE BOOK OF WOOD CARVING, Charles Marshall Sayers. Finest book for beginners discusses fundamentals and offers 34 designs. "Absolutely first rate . . . well thought out and well executed."–E. J. Tangerman. 118pp. 7¾ x 10⅝. 23654-4

ILLUSTRATED CATALOG OF CIVIL WAR MILITARY GOODS: Union Army Weapons, Insignia, Uniform Accessories, and Other Equipment, Schuyler, Hartley, and Graham. Rare, profusely illustrated 1846 catalog includes Union Army uniform and dress regulations, arms and ammunition, coats, insignia, flags, swords, rifles, etc. 226 illustrations. 160pp. 9 x 12. 24939-5

WOMEN'S FASHIONS OF THE EARLY 1900s: An Unabridged Republication of "New York Fashions, 1909," National Cloak & Suit Co. Rare catalog of mail-order fashions documents women's and children's clothing styles shortly after the turn of the century. Captions offer full descriptions, prices. Invaluable resource for fashion, costume historians. Approximately 725 illustrations. 128pp. 8⅜ x 11¼. 27276-1

THE 1912 AND 1915 GUSTAV STICKLEY FURNITURE CATALOGS, Gustav Stickley. With over 200 detailed illustrations and descriptions, these two catalogs are essential reading and reference materials and identification guides for Stickley furniture. Captions cite materials, dimensions and prices. 112pp. 6½ x 9¼. 26676-1

EARLY AMERICAN LOCOMOTIVES, John H. White, Jr. Finest locomotive engravings from early 19th century: historical (1804–74), main-line (after 1870), special, foreign, etc. 147 plates. 142pp. 11⅜ x 8¼. 22772-3

THE TALL SHIPS OF TODAY IN PHOTOGRAPHS, Frank O. Braynard. Lavishly illustrated tribute to nearly 100 majestic contemporary sailing vessels: Amerigo Vespucci, Clearwater, Constitution, Eagle, Mayflower, Sea Cloud, Victory, many more. Authoritative captions provide statistics, background on each ship. 190 black-and-white photographs and illustrations. Introduction. 128pp. 8⅞ x 11¾. 27163-3

LITTLE BOOK OF EARLY AMERICAN CRAFTS AND TRADES, Peter Stockham (ed.). 1807 children's book explains crafts and trades: baker, hatter, cooper, potter, and many others. 23 copperplate illustrations. 140pp. 4⅝ x 6. 23336-7

VICTORIAN FASHIONS AND COSTUMES FROM HARPER'S BAZAR, 1867–1898, Stella Blum (ed.). Day costumes, evening wear, sports clothes, shoes, hats, other accessories in over 1,000 detailed engravings. 320pp. 9⅜ x 12¼. 22990-4

GUSTAV STICKLEY, THE CRAFTSMAN, Mary Ann Smith. Superb study surveys broad scope of Stickley's achievement, especially in architecture. Design philosophy, rise and fall of the Craftsman empire, descriptions and floor plans for many Craftsman houses, more. 86 black-and-white halftones. 31 line illustrations. Introduction 208pp. 6½ x 9¼. 27210-9

THE LONG ISLAND RAIL ROAD IN EARLY PHOTOGRAPHS, Ron Ziel. Over 220 rare photos, informative text document origin (1844) and development of rail service on Long Island. Vintage views of early trains, locomotives, stations, passengers, crews, much more. Captions. 8⅞ x 11¾. 26301-0

VOYAGE OF THE LIBERDADE, Joshua Slocum. Great 19th-century mariner's thrilling, first-hand account of the wreck of his ship off South America, the 35-foot boat he built from the wreckage, and its remarkable voyage home. 128pp. 5⅜ x 8½. 40022-0

TEN BOOKS ON ARCHITECTURE, Vitruvius. The most important book ever written on architecture. Early Roman aesthetics, technology, classical orders, site selection, all other aspects. Morgan translation. 331pp. 5⅜ x 8½. 20645-9

THE HUMAN FIGURE IN MOTION, Eadweard Muybridge. More than 4,500 stopped-action photos, in action series, showing undraped men, women, children jumping, lying down, throwing, sitting, wrestling, carrying, etc. 390pp. 7⅞ x 10⅝. 20204-6 Clothbd.

TREES OF THE EASTERN AND CENTRAL UNITED STATES AND CANADA, William M. Harlow. Best one-volume guide to 140 trees. Full descriptions, woodlore, range, etc. Over 600 illustrations. Handy size. 288pp. 4½ x 6⅜. 20395-6

SONGS OF WESTERN BIRDS, Dr. Donald J. Borror. Complete song and call repertoire of 60 western species, including flycatchers, juncoes, cactus wrens, many more–includes fully illustrated booklet. Cassette and manual 99913-0

GROWING AND USING HERBS AND SPICES, Milo Miloradovich. Versatile handbook provides all the information needed for cultivation and use of all the herbs and spices available in North America. 4 illustrations. Index. Glossary. 236pp. 5⅜ x 8½. 25058-X

BIG BOOK OF MAZES AND LABYRINTHS, Walter Shepherd. 50 mazes and labyrinths in all–classical, solid, ripple, and more–in one great volume. Perfect inexpensive puzzler for clever youngsters. Full solutions. 112pp. 8⅛ x 11. 22951-3

PIANO TUNING, J. Cree Fischer. Clearest, best book for beginner, amateur. Simple repairs, raising dropped notes, tuning by easy method of flattened fifths. No previous skills needed. 4 illustrations. 201pp. 5⅜ x 8½. 23267-0

HINTS TO SINGERS, Lillian Nordica. Selecting the right teacher, developing confidence, overcoming stage fright, and many other important skills receive thoughtful discussion in this indispensible guide, written by a world-famous diva of four decades' experience. 96pp. 5⅜ x 8½. 40094-8

THE COMPLETE NONSENSE OF EDWARD LEAR, Edward Lear. All nonsense limericks, zany alphabets, Owl and Pussycat, songs, nonsense botany, etc., illustrated by Lear. Total of 320pp. 5⅜ x 8½. (Available in U.S. only.) 20167-8

VICTORIAN PARLOUR POETRY: An Annotated Anthology, Michael R. Turner. 117 gems by Longfellow, Tennyson, Browning, many lesser-known poets. "The Village Blacksmith," "Curfew Must Not Ring Tonight," "Only a Baby Small," dozens more, often difficult to find elsewhere. Index of poets, titles, first lines. xxiii + 325pp. 5⅝ x 8¼. 27044-0

DUBLINERS, James Joyce. Fifteen stories offer vivid, tightly focused observations of the lives of Dublin's poorer classes. At least one, "The Dead," is considered a masterpiece. Reprinted complete and unabridged from standard edition. 160pp. 5$\frac{3}{16}$ x 8¼. 26870-5

GREAT WEIRD TALES: 14 Stories by Lovecraft, Blackwood, Machen and Others, S. T. Joshi (ed.). 14 spellbinding tales, including "The Sin Eater," by Fiona McLeod, "The Eye Above the Mantel," by Frank Belknap Long, as well as renowned works by R. H. Barlow, Lord Dunsany, Arthur Machen, W. C. Morrow and eight other masters of the genre. 256pp. 5⅜ x 8½. (Available in U.S. only.) 40436-6

THE BOOK OF THE SACRED MAGIC OF ABRAMELIN THE MAGE, translated by S. MacGregor Mathers. Medieval manuscript of ceremonial magic. Basic document in Aleister Crowley, Golden Dawn groups. 268pp. 5⅜ x 8½. 23211-5

NEW RUSSIAN-ENGLISH AND ENGLISH-RUSSIAN DICTIONARY, M. A. O'Brien. This is a remarkably handy Russian dictionary, containing a surprising amount of information, including over 70,000 entries. 366pp. 4½ x 6⅛. 20208-9

HISTORIC HOMES OF THE AMERICAN PRESIDENTS, Second, Revised Edition, Irvin Haas. A traveler's guide to American Presidential homes, most open to the public, depicting and describing homes occupied by every American President from George Washington to George Bush. With visiting hours, admission charges, travel routes. 175 photographs. Index. 160pp. 8¼ x 11. 26751-2

NEW YORK IN THE FORTIES, Andreas Feininger. 162 brilliant photographs by the well-known photographer, formerly with *Life* magazine. Commuters, shoppers, Times Square at night, much else from city at its peak. Captions by John von Hartz. 181pp. 9¼ x 10¾. 23585-8

INDIAN SIGN LANGUAGE, William Tomkins. Over 525 signs developed by Sioux and other tribes. Written instructions and diagrams. Also 290 pictographs. 111pp. 6⅛ x 9¼. 22029-X

ANATOMY: A Complete Guide for Artists, Joseph Sheppard. A master of figure drawing shows artists how to render human anatomy convincingly. Over 460 illustrations. 224pp. 8⅜ x 11¼. 27279-6

MEDIEVAL CALLIGRAPHY: Its History and Technique, Marc Drogin. Spirited history, comprehensive instruction manual covers 13 styles (ca. 4th century through 15th). Excellent photographs; directions for duplicating medieval techniques with modern tools. 224pp. 8⅜ x 11¼. 26142-5

DRIED FLOWERS: How to Prepare Them, Sarah Whitlock and Martha Rankin. Complete instructions on how to use silica gel, meal and borax, perlite aggregate, sand and borax, glycerine and water to create attractive permanent flower arrangements. 12 illustrations. 32pp. 5⅜ x 8½. 21802-3

EASY-TO-MAKE BIRD FEEDERS FOR WOODWORKERS, Scott D. Campbell. Detailed, simple-to-use guide for designing, constructing, caring for and using feeders. Text, illustrations for 12 classic and contemporary designs. 96pp. 5⅜ x 8½. 25847-5

SCOTTISH WONDER TALES FROM MYTH AND LEGEND, Donald A. Mackenzie. 16 lively tales tell of giants rumbling down mountainsides, of a magic wand that turns stone pillars into warriors, of gods and goddesses, evil hags, powerful forces and more. 240pp. 5⅜ x 8½. 29677-6

THE HISTORY OF UNDERCLOTHES, C. Willett Cunnington and Phyllis Cunnington. Fascinating, well-documented survey covering six centuries of English undergarments, enhanced with over 100 illustrations: 12th-century laced-up bodice, footed long drawers (1795), 19th-century bustles, l9th-century corsets for men, Victorian "bust improvers," much more. 272pp. 5⅜ x 8¼. 27124-2

ARTS AND CRAFTS FURNITURE: The Complete Brooks Catalog of 1912, Brooks Manufacturing Co. Photos and detailed descriptions of more than 150 now very collectible furniture designs from the Arts and Crafts movement depict davenports, settees, buffets, desks, tables, chairs, bedsteads, dressers and more, all built of solid, quarter-sawed oak. Invaluable for students and enthusiasts of antiques, Americana and the decorative arts. 80pp. 6½ x 9¼. 27471-3

WILBUR AND ORVILLE: A Biography of the Wright Brothers, Fred Howard. Definitive, crisply written study tells the full story of the brothers' lives and work. A vividly written biography, unparalleled in scope and color, that also captures the spirit of an extraordinary era. 560pp. 6⅛ x 9¼. 40297-5

THE ARTS OF THE SAILOR: Knotting, Splicing and Ropework, Hervey Garrett Smith. Indispensable shipboard reference covers tools, basic knots and useful hitches; handsewing and canvas work, more. Over 100 illustrations. Delightful reading for sea lovers. 256pp. 5⅜ x 8½. 26440-8

FRANK LLOYD WRIGHT'S FALLINGWATER: The House and Its History, Second, Revised Edition, Donald Hoffmann. A total revision—both in text and illustrations—of the standard document on Fallingwater, the boldest, most personal architectural statement of Wright's mature years, updated with valuable new material from the recently opened Frank Lloyd Wright Archives. "Fascinating"—*The New York Times*. 116 illustrations. 128pp. 9¼ x 10¾. 27430-6

PHOTOGRAPHIC SKETCHBOOK OF THE CIVIL WAR, Alexander Gardner. 100 photos taken on field during the Civil War. Famous shots of Manassas Harper's Ferry, Lincoln, Richmond, slave pens, etc. 244pp. 10⅝ x 8¼.   22731-6

FIVE ACRES AND INDEPENDENCE, Maurice G. Kains. Great back-to-the-land classic explains basics of self-sufficient farming. The one book to get. 95 illustrations. 397pp. 5⅜ x 8½.   20974-1

SONGS OF EASTERN BIRDS, Dr. Donald J. Borror. Songs and calls of 60 species most common to eastern U.S.: warblers, woodpeckers, flycatchers, thrushes, larks, many more in high-quality recording.   Cassette and manual 99912-2

A MODERN HERBAL, Margaret Grieve. Much the fullest, most exact, most useful compilation of herbal material. Gigantic alphabetical encyclopedia, from aconite to zedoary, gives botanical information, medical properties, folklore, economic uses, much else. Indispensable to serious reader. 161 illustrations. 888pp. 6½ x 9¼. 2-vol. set. (Available in U.S. only.)   Vol. I: 22798-7
          Vol. II: 22799-5

HIDDEN TREASURE MAZE BOOK, Dave Phillips. Solve 34 challenging mazes accompanied by heroic tales of adventure. Evil dragons, people-eating plants, blood-thirsty giants, many more dangerous adversaries lurk at every twist and turn. 34 mazes, stories, solutions. 48pp. 8¼ x 11.   24566-7

LETTERS OF W. A. MOZART, Wolfgang A. Mozart. Remarkable letters show bawdy wit, humor, imagination, musical insights, contemporary musical world; includes some letters from Leopold Mozart. 276pp. 5⅜ x 8½.   22859-2

BASIC PRINCIPLES OF CLASSICAL BALLET, Agrippina Vaganova. Great Russian theoretician, teacher explains methods for teaching classical ballet. 118 illustrations. 175pp. 5⅜ x 8½.   22036-2

THE JUMPING FROG, Mark Twain. Revenge edition. The original story of The Celebrated Jumping Frog of Calaveras County, a hapless French translation, and Twain's hilarious "retranslation" from the French. 12 illustrations. 66pp. 5⅜ x 8½.
          22686-7

BEST REMEMBERED POEMS, Martin Gardner (ed.). The 126 poems in this superb collection of 19th- and 20th-century British and American verse range from Shelley's "To a Skylark" to the impassioned "Renascence" of Edna St. Vincent Millay and to Edward Lear's whimsical "The Owl and the Pussycat." 224pp. 5⅜ x 8½.
          27165-X

COMPLETE SONNETS, William Shakespeare. Over 150 exquisite poems deal with love, friendship, the tyranny of time, beauty's evanescence, death and other themes in language of remarkable power, precision and beauty. Glossary of archaic terms. 80pp. 5³⁄₁₆ x 8¼.   26686-9

THE BATTLES THAT CHANGED HISTORY, Fletcher Pratt. Eminent historian profiles 16 crucial conflicts, ancient to modern, that changed the course of civilization. 352pp. 5⅜ x 8½.   41129-X

THE WIT AND HUMOR OF OSCAR WILDE, Alvin Redman (ed.). More than 1,000 ripostes, paradoxes, wisecracks: Work is the curse of the drinking classes; I can resist everything except temptation; etc. 258pp. 5⅜ x 8½. 20602-5

SHAKESPEARE LEXICON AND QUOTATION DICTIONARY, Alexander Schmidt. Full definitions, locations, shades of meaning in every word in plays and poems. More than 50,000 exact quotations. 1,485pp. 6½ x 9¼. 2-vol. set.
Vol. 1: 22726-X
Vol. 2: 22727-8

SELECTED POEMS, Emily Dickinson. Over 100 best-known, best-loved poems by one of America's foremost poets, reprinted from authoritative early editions. No comparable edition at this price. Index of first lines. 64pp. 5³⁄₁₆ x 8¼. 26466-1

THE INSIDIOUS DR. FU-MANCHU, Sax Rohmer. The first of the popular mystery series introduces a pair of English detectives to their archnemesis, the diabolical Dr. Fu-Manchu. Flavorful atmosphere, fast-paced action, and colorful characters enliven this classic of the genre. 208pp. 5³⁄₁₆ x 8¼. 29898-1

THE MALLEUS MALEFICARUM OF KRAMER AND SPRENGER, translated by Montague Summers. Full text of most important witchhunter's "bible," used by both Catholics and Protestants. 278pp. 6⅝ x 10. 22802-9

SPANISH STORIES/CUENTOS ESPAÑOLES: A Dual-Language Book, Angel Flores (ed.). Unique format offers 13 great stories in Spanish by Cervantes, Borges, others. Faithful English translations on facing pages. 352pp. 5⅜ x 8½. 25399-6

GARDEN CITY, LONG ISLAND, IN EARLY PHOTOGRAPHS, 1869–1919, Mildred H. Smith. Handsome treasury of 118 vintage pictures, accompanied by carefully researched captions, document the Garden City Hotel fire (1899), the Vanderbilt Cup Race (1908), the first airmail flight departing from the Nassau Boulevard Aerodrome (1911), and much more. 96pp. 8⅞ x 11¾. 40669-5

OLD QUEENS, N.Y., IN EARLY PHOTOGRAPHS, Vincent F. Seyfried and William Asadorian. Over 160 rare photographs of Maspeth, Jamaica, Jackson Heights, and other areas. Vintage views of DeWitt Clinton mansion, 1939 World's Fair and more. Captions. 192pp. 8⅞ x 11. 26358-4

CAPTURED BY THE INDIANS: 15 Firsthand Accounts, 1750-1870, Frederick Drimmer. Astounding true historical accounts of grisly torture, bloody conflicts, relentless pursuits, miraculous escapes and more, by people who lived to tell the tale. 384pp. 5⅜ x 8½. 24901-8

THE WORLD'S GREAT SPEECHES (Fourth Enlarged Edition), Lewis Copeland, Lawrence W. Lamm, and Stephen J. McKenna. Nearly 300 speeches provide public speakers with a wealth of updated quotes and inspiration–from Pericles' funeral oration and William Jennings Bryan's "Cross of Gold Speech" to Malcolm X's powerful words on the Black Revolution and Earl of Spenser's tribute to his sister, Diana, Princess of Wales. 944pp. 5⅜ x 8⅜. 40903-1

THE BOOK OF THE SWORD, Sir Richard F. Burton. Great Victorian scholar/adventurer's eloquent, erudite history of the "queen of weapons"–from prehistory to early Roman Empire. Evolution and development of early swords, variations (sabre, broadsword, cutlass, scimitar, etc.), much more. 336pp. 6⅛ x 9¼. 25434-8

AUTOBIOGRAPHY: The Story of My Experiments with Truth, Mohandas K. Gandhi. Boyhood, legal studies, purification, the growth of the Satyagraha (nonviolent protest) movement. Critical, inspiring work of the man responsible for the freedom of India. 480pp. 5⅜ x 8½. (Available in U.S. only.)   24593-4

CELTIC MYTHS AND LEGENDS, T. W. Rolleston. Masterful retelling of Irish and Welsh stories and tales. Cuchulain, King Arthur, Deirdre, the Grail, many more. First paperback edition. 58 full-page illustrations. 512pp. 5⅜ x 8½.   26507-2

THE PRINCIPLES OF PSYCHOLOGY, William James. Famous long course complete, unabridged. Stream of thought, time perception, memory, experimental methods; great work decades ahead of its time. 94 figures. 1,391pp. 5⅜ x 8½. 2-vol. set.
Vol. I: 20381-6   Vol. II: 20382-4

THE WORLD AS WILL AND REPRESENTATION, Arthur Schopenhauer. Definitive English translation of Schopenhauer's life work, correcting more than 1,000 errors, omissions in earlier translations. Translated by E. F. J. Payne. Total of 1,269pp. 5⅜ x 8½. 2-vol. set.   Vol. 1: 21761-2   Vol. 2: 21762-0

MAGIC AND MYSTERY IN TIBET, Madame Alexandra David-Neel. Experiences among lamas, magicians, sages, sorcerers, Bonpa wizards. A true psychic discovery. 32 illustrations. 321pp. 5⅜ x 8½. (Available in U.S. only.)   22682-4

THE EGYPTIAN BOOK OF THE DEAD, E. A. Wallis Budge. Complete reproduction of Ani's papyrus, finest ever found. Full hieroglyphic text, interlinear transliteration, word-for-word translation, smooth translation. 533pp. 6½ x 9¼.   21866-X

MATHEMATICS FOR THE NONMATHEMATICIAN, Morris Kline. Detailed, college-level treatment of mathematics in cultural and historical context, with numerous exercises. Recommended Reading Lists. Tables. Numerous figures. 641pp. 5⅜ x 8½.   24823-2

PROBABILISTIC METHODS IN THE THEORY OF STRUCTURES, Isaac Elishakoff. Well-written introduction covers the elements of the theory of probability from two or more random variables, the reliability of such multivariable structures, the theory of random function, Monte Carlo methods of treating problems incapable of exact solution, and more. Examples. 502pp. 5⅜ x 8½.   40691-1

THE RIME OF THE ANCIENT MARINER, Gustave Doré, S. T. Coleridge. Doré's finest work; 34 plates capture moods, subtleties of poem. Flawless full-size reproductions printed on facing pages with authoritative text of poem. "Beautiful. Simply beautiful."–*Publisher's Weekly.* 77pp. 9¼ x 12.   22305-1

NORTH AMERICAN INDIAN DESIGNS FOR ARTISTS AND CRAFTSPEOPLE, Eva Wilson. Over 360 authentic copyright-free designs adapted from Navajo blankets, Hopi pottery, Sioux buffalo hides, more. Geometrics, symbolic figures, plant and animal motifs, etc. 128pp. 8⅜ x 11. (Not for sale in the United Kingdom.)   25341-4

SCULPTURE: Principles and Practice, Louis Slobodkin. Step-by-step approach to clay, plaster, metals, stone; classical and modern. 253 drawings, photos. 255pp. 8⅛ x 11.   22960-2

THE INFLUENCE OF SEA POWER UPON HISTORY, 1660–1783, A. T. Mahan. Influential classic of naval history and tactics still used as text in war colleges. First paperback edition. 4 maps. 24 battle plans. 640pp. 5⅜ x 8½.   25509-3

CATALOG OF DOVER BOOKS

THE STORY OF THE TITANIC AS TOLD BY ITS SURVIVORS, Jack Winocour (ed.). What it was really like. Panic, despair, shocking inefficiency, and a little heroism. More thrilling than any fictional account. 26 illustrations. 320pp. 5⅜ x 8½.
20610-6

FAIRY AND FOLK TALES OF THE IRISH PEASANTRY, William Butler Yeats (ed.). Treasury of 64 tales from the twilight world of Celtic myth and legend: "The Soul Cages," "The Kildare Pooka," "King O'Toole and his Goose," many more. Introduction and Notes by W. B. Yeats. 352pp. 5⅜ x 8½.
26941-8

BUDDHIST MAHAYANA TEXTS, E. B. Cowell and others (eds.). Superb, accurate translations of basic documents in Mahayana Buddhism, highly important in history of religions. The Buddha-karita of Asvaghosha, Larger Sukhavativyuha, more. 448pp. 5⅜ x 8½.
25552-2

ONE TWO THREE . . . INFINITY: Facts and Speculations of Science, George Gamow. Great physicist's fascinating, readable overview of contemporary science: number theory, relativity, fourth dimension, entropy, genes, atomic structure, much more. 128 illustrations. Index. 352pp. 5⅜ x 8½.
25664-2

EXPERIMENTATION AND MEASUREMENT, W. J. Youden. Introductory manual explains laws of measurement in simple terms and offers tips for achieving accuracy and minimizing errors. Mathematics of measurement, use of instruments, experimenting with machines. 1994 edition. Foreword. Preface. Introduction. Epilogue. Selected Readings. Glossary. Index. Tables and figures. 128pp. 5⅜ x 8½.   40451-X

DALÍ ON MODERN ART: The Cuckolds of Antiquated Modern Art, Salvador Dalí. Influential painter skewers modern art and its practitioners. Outrageous evaluations of Picasso, Cézanne, Turner, more. 15 renderings of paintings discussed. 44 calligraphic decorations by Dalí. 96pp. 5⅜ x 8½. (Available in U.S. only.)   29220-7

ANTIQUE PLAYING CARDS: A Pictorial History, Henry René D'Allemagne. Over 900 elaborate, decorative images from rare playing cards (14th–20th centuries): Bacchus, death, dancing dogs, hunting scenes, royal coats of arms, players cheating, much more. 96pp. 9¼ x 12¼.
29265-7

MAKING FURNITURE MASTERPIECES: 30 Projects with Measured Drawings, Franklin H. Gottshall. Step-by-step instructions, illustrations for constructing handsome, useful pieces, among them a Sheraton desk, Chippendale chair, Spanish desk, Queen Anne table and a William and Mary dressing mirror. 224pp. 8¼ x 11¼.
29338-6

THE FOSSIL BOOK: A Record of Prehistoric Life, Patricia V. Rich et al. Profusely illustrated definitive guide covers everything from single-celled organisms and dinosaurs to birds and mammals and the interplay between climate and man. Over 1,500 illustrations. 760pp. 7½ x 10⅛.
29371-8

Paperbound unless otherwise indicated. Available at your book dealer, online at **www.dover-publications.com**, or by writing to Dept. GI, Dover Publications, Inc., 31 East 2nd Street, Mineola, NY 11501. For current price information or for free catalogues (please indicate field of interest), write to Dover Publications or log on to **www.doverpublications.com** and see every Dover book in print. Dover publishes more than 500 books each year on science, elementary and advanced mathematics, biology, music, art, literary history, social sciences, and other areas.